THE TREE OF LIFE

READING PROVERBS TODAY

Graeme Goldsworthy

PRESS

Anglican Information Office
Sydney NSW 2000

PUBLISHED JUNE 1993

BY THE ANGLICAN INFORMATION OFFICE
ST. ANDREW'S HOUSE, SYDNEY SQUARE 2000

NATIONAL LIBRARY OF AUSTRALIA
ISBN 0 949108 44 8

PRINTED IN AUSTRALIA BY
Southwood Press Pty. Ltd., Sydney

Contents

Foreword

The ideal author for this series is one who is both a scholar and pastor. Such persons are very difficult to find. Dr Graeme Goldsworthy is such an author. He has for many years engaged in academic study of the Wisdom Literature of the Old Testament, while at the same time being engaged in ongoing pastoral ministry.

The author's grasp of the overall message and thematic structure of Proverbs will be evident on every page. But Dr Goldsworthy is also a great scholar of biblical theology. His insights into Proverbs are carefully integrated with the overall message of the Scriptures. His easy and readable style disguises the depth of his scholarship and his extensive reflection on the Proverbs, their place in the Scriptures and their meaning for us today.

Dr Paul Barnett
Series Editor
(Bishop of North Sydney)

Introduction:
A guide for the uninitiated

Blessed is the man who finds wisdom,
the man who gains understanding . . .
She is a tree of life to those who embrace her;
those who lay hold of her will be blessed. (Prov 3:13,18)

This book is a guide to the Book of Proverbs, written with the ordinary Christian reader in mind. My intention is to provide an introductory commentary that avoids, as far as possible, technical matters that the theologically untrained may find off-putting. I want to make Proverbs accessible to Christians so that they can read it as Christian Scripture in the light of the gospel. To achieve this I have included three things.

The first is an introduction to the idea of wisdom as it emerged in ancient Israel and as it eventually led to the production of the wisdom literature, including the Book of Proverbs. Chapters 1 to 4 will deal with the biblical background to the human task of gaining knowledge and understanding the world and our place in it. We will meet with the purposes of God in creating humankind in his image and with the effects of sin on human thought and reason. We will look at the loving plan of God to restore all things through his plan of redemption and how this bears on the way the people of God should use their minds. Finally, we will consider the formation and purpose of the Book of Proverbs as an expression of the redeemed mind reflecting on life in this world.

A second feature of this book is the selection of nine representative passages from the Book of Proverbs for special consideration. There are unique problems that face anyone attempting to write a commentary on Proverbs. First, there is no story sequence or narrative to provide some sort of unity. Furthermore, whatever structure exists in the whole has only the most indirect and flimsy relationship to the significance of the individual parts; the bulk of the book consists of one-sentence sayings that are quite independent of each other. So, a number of options are open to us for a commentary. We could pursue the normal "exegetical" pattern of a section-by-section and verse-by-verse analysis of the text. As important as this approach to any part of the Bible is, it does not open up Proverbs to the reader who wants to understand the book without a lot of technical detail. Another approach would be to take themes and examine the text for its treatment of them. The disadvantage of this is that it ignores the way Proverbs was actually put together as a whole book that came to be recognised as part of Holy Scripture. I have chosen a third option that I hope will satisfy a number of conditions, concentrating on sections of the book while at the same time providing essentially verse-by-verse commentary of the whole.

So, the third element of this book is a complete commentary at a basic level. My aim is to provide enough comment to make the meaning of the text plain without including a lot of technical detail about the linguistics or form. The reader should understand, however, that the key to the reading of Proverbs as Christian Scripture is discussed only in the sections dealing with the passages chosen for more extensive comment. Therefore, to get the most out of this book you will need to read it as a whole rather than use it as a reference book for comment on individual passages.

Reading Proverbs as Christian Scripture

My main aim in this book is to give some guidelines on the reading of Proverbs as Christian Scripture. Any book of the Old Testament needs to be read in the light of the coming of

Jesus Christ who is the climax of the revelation of God. Proverbs is no exception. However directly applicable to the present the book may seem, it is a mistake to think that its relationship to us is self-evident.

In order to open up the nature of Proverbs and its Christian application, I have chosen nine representative passages and attempted to show both the original meaning and the present Christian significance of them. These passages were chosen on the basis of their content and their form, so that a realistic cross-section of the whole book comes under scrutiny in this way.

These representative passages will be dealt with under four headings. The first is *Description*. Here we will look in general terms at the way the author or editor of Proverbs has actually shaped the material as a piece of literature. Then under *Text* I will give a verse-by verse commentary on the meaning that the words convey. *Function* will look at the meaning of the passage as a whole and its contribution to the message of Proverbs. Finally, the section called *Testimony to Christ* will examine the connection between the teaching of the passage and the gospel. The assumption is made that all Old Testament Scripture testifies to Christ (see Jn 5:39). Consequently, the relationship of an Old Testament passage to Christ is the precondition for knowing how the passage applies to us as twentieth-century Christians.

Reading Proverbs as Christian Scripture is a rewarding exercise. It sharpens our perceptions of what the renewing of our minds through the gospel involves (see Eph 4:21-24; Rom 12:1-2). It warns us against the mistaken piety that makes a false distinction between the practical and the theoretical. It encourages us in the responsible use of our God-given faculties of thought and reason. It gives important perspectives on the question of how God guides us. Perhaps most importantly, it foreshadows the perfect blend of divine and human wisdom revealed in Christ. In this we come face to face with God's grace and our task which are at the heart of understanding how we should seek to live as God's people in this world.

1

It all began with Adam

I think it's a horse

Anyone could be excused for wondering what Proverbs has to do with Adam and a horse. But look at it like this: when God made the first human pair they had a unique relationship to the Creator; they were made in his image, a gift that no other creature possessed (see Gen 1:26-27). Whatever the image of God consists of, we see it being expressed partly in the task that God gave the humans: "Be fruitful and increase in number; fill the earth and subdue it. Rule over the fish of the sea and the birds of the air and over every living creature that moves on the ground" (Gen 1:28). Have you ever tried to imagine what it would have been like to have been the newly created couple as they woke to the world and to each other? They were rational, thinking beings, yet without experience in the new intellectual adventure that was theirs.

Now consider that in Genesis 2 we see the creation of humankind from a different perspective. Here the emphasis is on the way the man and the woman will complement each other. The narrative tells of God bringing the animals to Adam to see what he would name them (v. 19). Imagine Adam scratching his head and saying, "I wonder what I ought to name this one? I think it looks like a horse so I will name it 'horse.'" I do not actually believe for a moment that is what the story intends; it is more concerned with the need for a suitable helper for the man, a need that none of the animals could meet. Again, I do not think that the narrative is meant to imply that God did not know who would be Adam's partner; Genesis 1 tells us that God's intention was the creation of the human species as male and female. In Genesis 2 the emphasis is on the complementary roles of male and female.

Now let us put these two aspects of the creation story together. It belongs to our humanness that we are commissioned by God to take charge of the world, and to do that we have to know and understand it. Naming the animals shows a measure of control over them. It also shows that it belongs to being human to examine, classify and name things. In other words, God gave us intelligence and reasoning powers that none of the animals have. He made us capable of getting knowledge by using our senses, and of processing or organising that knowledge into a coherent whole. We tend to take for granted the whole business of using our minds, or not using them as the case may be. The human mind with its powers of reasoning is one of the greatest gifts God gave to us. But we need to be reminded of this fact, and we need to learn how to apply our minds to the business of living.

There are two sources of knowledge referred to in the creation narratives: the creation and the Creator. Natural knowledge comes from what is to be found in the world around us. Supernatural knowledge comes from the spiritual world, and is beyond our ability as humans to find out. God must communicate as much of this as he wants us to have. The evidence for the existence of God that is built into the creation is part of natural truth (see Rom 1:19-20). However, we see in Genesis 1:28-30 that God first communicates to the humans by his word. He gives them an understanding of what their task is and how they relate to God, to each other and to the world. This is the framework of supernatural truth by which they will understand the significance of all the natural facts that they will discover through their senses. Humans do not reason properly unless they start with God's word in order to understand all the facts gathered through the senses.

In other words, it is central to our God-given human task that we seek after knowledge and wisdom. The creation stories remind us that God is the source of all truth. The truth that we discover by using our senses is truth about a reality that is entirely of God's making. But this reality that is open to our senses is only a part of the total reality. Beyond it there is a spiritual realm, including God and created spiritual beings. There is evidence for this spiritual realm in the natural world, but it is essentially outside our ability to discover. The two realms are part of one reality and are bound up with one another. The ultimate purpose and meaning of everything, natural and supernatural, is determined by God.

This means that the real and eternal significance of each part of the creation can only be described in relation to the God who made it. Human beings were intended to understand every fact discovered by the senses (often called *empirical knowledge*) in the light of the word which God spoke (*revealed knowledge*). It is important to note that right from the very start God made it clear that part of being human was to be a knowledge-gatherer. He also made it clear that true wisdom understands all facts in the light of the eternal truth which God must reveal. Thus, every fact that we discover with our senses is finally understood correctly only because we see it as a fact interpreted by God. The real and eternal significance of anything is the significance that God gives it in his eternal purposes. As we shall see, this is what Proverbs means when it says, "The fear of the Lord is the beginning of knowledge" (1:7).

He loves me, he loves me not . . .

So, Genesis tells us, the human pair began the task of learning about the world and of taking charge of it. But the biblical story turns quickly to the temptation in the Garden of Eden (see Gen 3:1-7). Here we see the serpent suggesting to the woman that God really does not reveal the truth when he speaks. By accusing God of lying, the serpent sows the seed of the most damaging idea that a person can have: that God's interpretation of reality is deliberately falsified. The implication is that God cannot be trusted, and the invitation is thus given to begin the process of understanding reality from a purely human-centred point of view. The serpent suggests that the humans have to decide whether God speaks to them out of love or hatred. Their decision is that God has not been honest with them about the true nature of things. In other words, they take to themselves the role of the final authority in deciding what is right or wrong, true or false.

From this point on, rebellion against the authority of God's word is the hallmark of human sin. From this point on, humans seek to understand the world and their role in it without any reference to the revelation of God in his word. The author of all truth is now simply ignored as the human race engages the intellectual task alone. God is seen by humans to be unloving and to be acting out of self-interest that does not want the good of humankind.

God-think or serpent-think?

Genesis 1 to 3 shows us that there are only two possible ways to approach the interpretation of reality: God's way or the serpent's. The human pair chose the serpent's interpretation. Adam and Eve's removal from the paradise Garden of Eden speaks to us of a catastrophic fall from the true human condition. Humans were meant to be gatherers of facts in fellowship with a loving Creator who reveals by his word the ultimate meaning of all facts. But now there is no longer a partnership with the One who speaks that word which is necessary if humanity is to know the purpose and meaning of life. So rebellious is the attitude of fallen humankind that people dismiss the removal from Eden as myth and seek other explanations for the existence of evil and disruption in our world.

Since Eden, all over the world, as different groups of people developed distinctive cultures, spoke different languages and worshipped different gods, the pursuit of knowledge has gone on. In all cultures people have reflected on and learned from their experiences. They have sinfully interpreted the things they learned as due to this spirit or that local god, but learn they did. Within the warped framework of false religions they reasoned and planned and invented, and looked for some underlying plan or order in the whole universe. Ancient man saw imperfections in himself and the universe in terms of the spirits of nature or the caprice of the gods. Modern man sees such imperfections as natural and as evidence of an unfinished process. The rebellion deep within and the deathly veil drawn over the conscience has prevented people in all ages from acknowledging their corporate guilt and offensiveness to God, the Holy One and Creator Lord.

So, within our warped and rebellious mind-sets, people of all races and ages have gathered a wisdom which is deceptively good. It works because we learn from our common experience of the same world. Always there has been this search for understanding so that we as humans might better control the creation for our own good. Only now are we beginning to understand the folly of human wisdom as we see the fragility of our earth, our life-support

11

system, in a hostile environment of an uninhabitable space. Yet, without the revelation of God received by regenerate minds, humans still think like the serpent.

From the beginning of human society, people have observed and thought and crystallised into words their ideas about their experiences. Memorable experiences were reflected upon and sometimes a statement was made which would be repeated and passed on so as to preserve the meaning of that experience. In time the original experience was forgotten, while the saying lived on to be applied here and there to other people's experiences.

Love's labours not lost

In the biblical world outside Eden, in Genesis 4 to 11, we see two kinds of human existence unfolding. There is, on one hand, the continuing growth of human wickedness as the effect of rebellion against God. It takes us from Cain, the first murderer, to the vicious Lamech, and then to the evil that finally provokes God to destroy the world with the flood. On the other hand, there is a line of people among whom God is seen to be graciously acting to restore them to fellowship with himself. This line takes us from Seth to Noah, then from Shem to Abraham.

It is important to realise that the Bible concentrates on the activity of God in bringing about a restoration of the human race and of the creation at large. The central message of Scripture is salvation, which is God acting in unconditional love to restore his creation to the right relationship with himself. The human story in the Bible is related to this because people are the central objects of God's acts and revelation of salvation, but the human story always remains secondary to the story of what God is doing. The Bible is a book about God first, and only then is it a book about people.

This means that we do not have much information in the Bible on the day-by-day existence of the ordinary people who are at the centre of God's actions. The major saving events – the call of Abraham, the exodus of Israel from Egypt, the possession of Canaan, and the Davidic monarchy in Jerusalem – are spread over a period of eight or nine hundred years. Clearly, then, most Israelites lived and died without ever witnessing one of these events which make up the bulk of Old Testament history. Yet life went on and the culture of the people developed, including the process of gaining knowledge about life. The human story of the quest for wisdom and knowledge in Israel is not narrated in any great detail, so we must to some extent learn to read between the lines of the main story of God's acts if we are to have some idea of the emergence of wisdom.

2

That's what
they say

Human wisdom in the making

Gary Larson, creator of the "Far Side" cartoons, has a drawing in which a man sits in a small room talking on a telephone and is surrounded by other telephones each labelled "They." A woman stands at the door and exclaims: "You! Bernie Horowitz, so you're the 'They' in 'That's what they say.'" Larson plays on the fact that we all recognise the claim to authority in the assertion, "They say . . .," and yet no one thinks to try to identify the credentials of this authority. "They say . . ." means that the statement in question has found general acceptance in society and thus has the authority of an implied majority consent.

This anonymous authority is as old as the Bible. In Genesis 10:9 we read of Nimrod, "He was a mighty hunter before the Lord; that is why it is said, 'Like Nimrod, a mighty hunter before the Lord.'" There are other "They say . . ." or similar sayings in the Bible, for example, 1 Samuel 10:12; 19:24; and 2 Samuel 5:8.

If you care to look in a good library you should be able to find similar wisdom sayings and proverbs of many cultures, both ancient and modern. It is simply a part of life that, as humans, we gather sayings of wisdom that pass into the oral and written literature of our various racial and national groups. Much of the wisdom of the ancient Israelites has been conveniently gathered for us in the biblical books of Proverbs, Job and Ecclesiastes. Later Hebrew wisdom, much of it heavily influenced by Greek culture, is found in the non-biblical books of Jesus ben Sirach (Ecclesiasticus), The Wisdom of Solomon, and others.

Given the universal human need to know the world and how to live successfully in it, we may suppose that the ancient Hebrews were no different from other nations who distilled from experience the wisdom to live a rewarding life. Every day for every individual was a new day with new experiences. From time to time, someone would reflect on an experience and coin a saying to enshrine the lesson learned. Some of these sayings would be related to an inner circle, to the family or common interest group. Many of these sayings would probably die out or not be noticed by the community at large. Others would relate to the common life and eventually find a place in the oral wisdom of that community. In time, a body of folk wisdom with the authority of "They say. . ." grew and was written down by various scribes.

Most of the short wise sayings became accepted for their applicability to different situations and were separated from the original experiences that generated them. But because these sayings originated in relation to specific experiences, they could not be applied like general laws; they had to be scrutinised for their ability to guide behaviour in other situations. Thus, becoming wise included learning the skill of applying wise sayings in any given situation.

Hebrew society developed as a *covenant* society. By this we mean that its origins and growth were always in relation to the activity of God who summoned Abraham, the father of the nation, and made a covenant with him (see Gen 12:1-3; 15:1-17). According to this covenant, God led Abraham's descendants through a redemptive experience, the exodus from Egypt, that included giving them guidance on the way his redeemed people were to live. The Sinai covenant or law, understood in the light of the exodus experience, became the chief influence on the ordinary life of all Israelites (see Ex 19, 20 and 24).

Now we can draw a parallel between the life of the redeemed Israelites in the promised land, and the life of Adam and Eve in Eden. In Eden the people of God had to learn about the world and life in it by using their senses and their powers of reason. This process was governed by what God had revealed through his word. In like manner, Israel, as the people of God, also had the revealing word of God that interpreted their existence in relation to the covenant and the redeeming acts of God. Thus, within this framework, the nation, and individual Israelites, continued the never-ending human activity of gathering knowledge.

There's the outline, now colour in the human bits

An important feature of the Bible is that it is story: it has a beginning, and it develops towards an end. The story is, as I have already stressed, mainly the story of what God does. But, if this activity of God is the framework, or the reference point, for the human activity of thinking about the facts of living and understanding the meaning of it all, how did people get on while the story was developing?

Let us consider the biblical story bit by bit. Starting with Abraham as the father of the Israelite nation that God chose as his special people, what framework did he have within which to do his thinking? How did that framework develop? Abraham was given what we call the covenant promises, namely, that his descendants would be a great nation of God's people living in the promised land. This nation would be also the means of God's purposes of blessing reaching all the nations of the world (see Gen 12:1-3). This was fairly basic stuff and not much basis for understanding the world, but it was enough to enable the early Hebrews to know God, to be saved by faith (see Rom 4 and Gal 3) and to know something of the ultimate meaning of their life and the world.

Later, in the time of Moses, the descendants of Abraham received significant revelation of the meaning of redemption (through the exodus) and the structure of the redeemed life (through the law of Sinai). Within this framework they had a much clearer idea of God's working and how they should respond to him. This response, which the Bible refers to generally as "the fear of the Lord" (e.g. Ex 20:20; Deut 6:2, 24; 10:12) included the task of understanding their life and gaining wisdom. However, Israel did not have the completed picture until she was in the promised land and living as a redeemed people under the rule of God.

This rule of God was represented to Israel in several important ways. First, by the king who was meant to reflect the absolute but loving shepherd-role of God among his people. Second, there was the temple. Here the people learned that their relationship with God was regulated by the priestly ministry through which they, as sinners, were reconciled to God. Third, there was the continuing ministry of the prophets who represented the supreme authority of the word of God in the life of God's people. Thus, not until King Solomon had built the temple in Jerusalem was the framework of revelation complete.

It is not surprising, then, that although there was wisdom activity in the life of the Hebrews from earliest times, Solomon marked the flowering of the wisdom of the nation in a way unprecedented in Israel or in any other nation. Although Moses had been trained in the wisdom of Egypt (see Acts 7:22), it seems there was little activity in Israel in reflecting on wisdom or in committing it to writing until the time of Solomon. Solomon was the first Israelite to be marked out for his wisdom activity (see 1 Ki 3:5-28; 4:29-34; 10:1-9). Moreover, the whole account of Solomon's life in 1 Kings chapters 3 to 10 is concerned with how his wisdom was expressed and the fruit it bore. At the centre of Solomon's wise life is the building of the temple and the reflection on the vital role it played in the relationship of God to his people; here is the heart of what it means to fear the Lord (see 1 Ki 8:22-61).

This is not to say that wisdom was not developing all the while before Solomon. Remember, it began with Adam and Eve and continued in the life of people outside the Garden of Eden. The common features of human wisdom in every culture, as well as what we know of the progress of Israel as a nation, enable us to suggest some developments before Solomon came on the scene. It is highly likely that in ancient Israel wisdom began with the ordinary people in their daily lives. Over the centuries a practical folk wisdom would have been accumulated and passed on by word of mouth from generation to generation.

Then there would have been the formation of wisdom that reflected on the right application of the law and the knowledge of God's saving acts (see Dt 6:20-25). Much of this would have developed in family life, especially in the instruction of children. Life demanded also that children be instructed in everyday matters not specifically mentioned in the laws and statutes; human experience would be applied to daily life as parents and others gave guidance to the young.

In time, as the life of the nation settled and became more complex in its structures, there would have been the need to instruct those who were to take on specific responsibilities of leadership in the community. While there is little direct evidence of schools for the future ruling elite in Israel, much of the material in the book of Proverbs makes most sense if it had been used first in such schools.

The animals won't stand still

As Adam had been given the task of naming the animals, we may presume that in a perfect world he could exercise his God-given rule over them to assemble them and get them to stand still while he examined them. Adam would have had no trouble in relating the facts of his investigations to the word of God so that he could fit all things of his experience into the reality of God's ordered universe. But once human rebellion provoked the judgment of God the world was a different place. Human beings refused to acknowledge the true state of affairs and ceased to reason in the light of God's word.

Adam's world inside Eden was orderly and perfect. Ours is a world outside Eden in which all relationships have been dislocated and distorted. Not only is there a problem with the way the universe functions, but our minds refuse to acknowledge what has gone wrong. Israel's wisdom, then, had to take account of several factors that influenced the way the world was understood. It is clear from the beginning of human life outside the Garden of Eden that God preserved enough order in his creation to enable human life to continue. Yet there is a constant frustration built into our existence that confuses the meaning of things (see Rom 8:19-22). Part of wisdom is learning to perceive the extent of order and the extent of confusion in it all.

Another part of wisdom is coming to know the limitations of wisdom. Two things limit our grasp on total reality. The first is our humanness. God never intended human beings, even when in perfect fellowship with him, to know all things in the way he himself knows them (see Gen 2:16). Second, our sinful rebellion against God has made us unable to know properly even those things that God intended for us to know. This disorder includes the fact that sin caused all relationships to be fractured. When we get out into the world to carry on the task of investigating it and knowing it, unlike Adam, the animals won't stand still for us. Yes, reality is still relatively ordered, but God's judgment on our rebellion means that there is a fuzziness to the order. Sometimes there is such an impenetrable mist that we are faced with situations for which there seems no explanation.

There are more things in heaven and earth . . .

If we accept the serpent's interpretation of reality, we must assume that we are able to understand all things through what our senses perceive. There can be no mysteries, no knowable God who is in any way connected to reality or its meaning, no knowledge for which we are dependent upon revelation from a higher being. But the Bible tells us what we really already know in our hearts: that we are dependent on the One who is the creator of all and Lord over all. The biblical wisdom books emphasise different aspects of human knowledge and together provide us with a comprehensive picture of the wisdom that is available to us.

The Book of Proverbs contains the kind of wisdom that stresses the existing order of things that God maintains in his goodness. Though it contains a number of sayings that recognise the limits of human wisdom and the right of God to do the unpredictable, Proverbs is mainly practical wisdom. It speaks of daily life and of common human relationships in the family, in education, in the neighbourhood, and in commercial activities. Its main assumption is the preservation of a perceptible order in the universe despite the confusion due to sin.

It is mainly in the Book of Job that we see a concern for the mystery in the order of the universe, so that for some things there is no rational answer. When we recognise this fact we are thrown onto God's love and mercy in trust that he does what is right. Such reflective wisdom is found in all cultures. It seems to lend itself more readily to longer, often poetic, forms of literature. It seeks to examine the complexities of human existence in relation to eternal realities, to God and his purposes. It acknowledges that human beings are small and that there is an area of reality that is shrouded in mystery but without which life and its meaning cannot be fully explained.

3

Solomon and Proverbs

We have seen that Solomon's wisdom was not a totally new thing. Behind it lay the whole intellectual adventure of the human race, and of the Israelite nation in particular. We have also seen that the relative lateness of the emergence of this flowering of Israelite wisdom may be explained by the relationship of true human wisdom to the revelation of the wisdom of God. This revelation involved a process within the history of the Israelite people. Thus, there had to be some delay in the beginning of the reflection on experience until there was a measure of completeness about the revelation. Only then could human wisdom activity flourish.

The Bible shows that human history as a whole is linked to the specific history of Israel as the chosen nation. God is shown to be working through Israel to bring all things in creation back into harmony with himself. We might wonder why the ancient Babylonians and Egyptians produced wisdom literature much earlier than the Israelites. Israel was, of course, a much younger nation with a less developed culture than its neighbours. It also experienced a unique relationship to God. What Adam and Eve had lost was beginning to be restored through a nation called to represent the whole human race in the process of redemption and renewal. We know from the wider message of the Bible that this redemptive work was finally achieved in the person and work of a particular Israelite named Jesus of Nazareth. How then does Solomon relate to the ministry of Jesus?

When we look beyond the actual historical events to their significance as told to Israel by the prophetic word, we find the following aspects which make up the way of salvation. The call of God came to his people who were in bondage in Egypt to a power that was opposed to God. In response to this bondage, God acted to show that his commitment to his chosen people still stood. This action involved the powerful rescue of the people in the exodus from their alien captivity. The rescued people are then bonded to God in the covenant of Sinai. Then they are brought into the place which God has promised them so that they might be free to relate to God without hindrance. The focus of this place is the city of Jerusalem and the temple. The focus of the rule of God becomes a line of human agents chosen to reflect the kingship of God among his chosen people. These were first the judges and then the kings. Solomon emerges as the king at the point at which the pattern of redemption is completed.

This means that the framework for understanding reality is complete by the time of Proverbs. It is still only the shadow of the true framework of God's word yet to come in the flesh as Jesus, but the shadow nevertheless reveals the complete structure or pattern of God's work of re-creation or regeneration. The "fear of the Lord" means the acceptance of God's word that interprets the critical events of Israel's history as God's acts to redeem Israel. It means a reverent response of faith to the God who thus shows himself to be the Redeemer.

We must not think of the intellectual coming of age of the covenant people as a kind of graduation from outdated religious ideas. That is the way the modern secular mind thinks about what happened in the intellectual movement of the eighteenth century that is called the Enlightenment. This marked the emergence of the post-Christian age in which the Christian faith was regarded more as superstition than as an acceptable and rational view of reality. Simply put, the spirit of the Enlightenment was to accept the serpent's interpretation of reality rather than God's. People thought of the Enlightenment as humanity coming of age and learning to do without the crutches of religion. But ancient Israel's coming of age meant that they possessed the completed framework of revelation that gave them a comprehensive view of reality. With this framework in place, the responsible "adult" task of gaining knowledge and wisdom could proceed apace.

Solomon foreshadows Jesus who would be the one who perfectly expresses the human activity of gaining wisdom and living by it. The revelation of God is the gift of the knowledge of the wisdom of God. This gift requires that the recipient engages in the responsible human task of wisdom. The author of 1 Kings seems determined to present Solomon and his wisdom achievements in as clear a light as possible before ever looking at the dark side of Solomon's behaviour. With the history of God's redemptive acts behind him, Solomon represents the people of God. They reflect on their existence in the light of the whole process from creation to new creation, and of the redemptive work of God to bring his people into his everlasting kingdom.

When David is about to die he charges Solomon to be obedient to the Lord and then repeats the promises of God to the royal line of David (1 Ki 2:1-4). In a way, this promise, first given by the prophet Nathan in 2 Samuel 7:4-16, sums up all God's plans for the salvation of his people. Solomon's request for an understanding mind to govern the people meets with the Lord's approval, and the king is consequently granted riches and honour in addition (1 Ki 3:5-14). The general theme of 1 Kings 3 to 10 is this wisdom of Solomon in action. First there is his handling of the case of the two prostitutes in their dispute over the baby (1 Ki 3:16-28). Then in 1 Kings 4:1-28 there are some details of the people of the kingdom that highlight the grandeur of the nation's organisation, the safety and prosperity of the people, and the fulfilment of the covenant promises of God. Solomon's wisdom is then compared with the wisdom of the wise ones of the surrounding nations and declared to be superior (1 Ki 4:29-34).

Solomon's building of the temple in Jerusalem is also regarded as an aspect of wisdom. Hiram of Tyre recognises this (1 Ki 5:7) and the author re-emphasises it in 1 Kings 5:12. Solomon's prayer of dedication is a theological summary of the significance of the building of the temple (1 Ki 8:23-53). The temple represents the presence of God among his people who are now settled and established in the promised land. At its heart is the expressiveness of the sacrificial system and the priestly office by which the nation and its individuals know reconciliation with God through the forgiveness of sins. It is here that they come to express their fellowship with a merciful and loving God who has created and redeemed them for himself. At the temple the Israelites are reminded of their role in God's purposes for the nations of the world. Solomon's prayer reflects on the covenant promise to Abraham that all the nations of the world will be blessed through this people (cf. Gen 12:2-3). It also anticipates the vision of the later prophets of a glorified temple on Mount Zion to which all the nations will come to find salvation. In short, here in Solomon's temple is the visible revelation of the meaning of the universe and of the specific meaning of human existence within that universe. That is the wisdom of God upon which all human wisdom depends.

For a Christian reading and interpretation of Proverbs this theological framework to wisdom and the significance of Solomon is important. This fact will emerge more clearly as we go on to consider the actual text, but we should remind ourselves often that the framework of the "fear of the Lord" that Proverbs itself testifies to (Prov 1:7) points us to the completed revelation of God in Jesus Christ. Every aspect of the Old Testament pattern of redemption from Abraham to Solomon, not to mention the underlying significance of the creation, has it final revelation in the person and work of Jesus. To interpret Proverbs in the light of the gospel is not to engage in some wild and fanciful spiritualising, but only to follow the example of Jesus himself and that of the New Testament.

Jesus' assertions about his role as the fulfiller of the Old Testament should sensitise us to the many ways that the New Testament sees this fulfilment taking place. It is not the purpose of this brief introduction to Proverbs to give a comprehensive description of the correspondences between the two Testaments. However, we have noted the significance of both the temple and Solomon as central to the climax of redemptive revelation within the history of Israel. It would therefore reward us greatly to consider how Jesus comes as the one who is greater than Solomon (see Mt 12:42), and is himself the new and living temple of God (see Jn 2:21). Jesus fulfils the role of the temple by being in his own person the place where God and humanity meet. Within his person he fulfils the priestly role of the one who mediates reconciliation with God on the grounds of an acceptable sacrifice for sin. As the true and representative Israelite, Jesus embodies the promises of God to David. The covenant promises to the descendants of Abraham are fulfilled in the resurrection of Jesus. In that event a new humanity that conforms to the will and purpose of God emerges (see Acts 2:30-32; 13:32-33; Rom 1:4; Heb 13:20). The meaning of the universe and of human existence is given its definitive statement in the death and resurrection of Jesus. Thus the gospel becomes the only framework within which we can carry on the human task of gathering and interpreting facts in the light of eternity.

4

Getting to know Proverbs

By whom and when?

You might think it unnecessary to ask the question about who wrote Proverbs since the book begins with the words, "The proverbs of Solomon son of David, king of Israel." But as we look further in the book we will find another reference to Solomon in 10:1, and then in 25:1 a reference to the proverbs of Solomon that were copied by Hezekiah's men. Chapter 30 is attributed to a man called Agur, and chapter 31 to King Lemuel. Clearly Solomon did not write it all.

In 1 Kings 4:32-33 we are told that Solomon was a prolific writer of proverbs (3000 of them) and a composer of songs (1005). The history of wisdom and the clear biblical evidence of Solomon's formative influence on the wisdom movement in Israel removes any reason to doubt the significant role of Solomon in the production of the book of Proverbs. What, then, does it mean to say Solomon wrote the proverbs that are given under his name? The very nature of wisdom would suggest that it is unlikely that Solomon could just decide to write some proverbs when the mood took him. Unless you already have the whole background of experiences, and apt sayings to go with them, you can't sit down and say, "I'm now going to write some proverbs." By its nature a proverb is more something that happens to us, or at least the experience behind it is. It would take time for the saying to become isolated from the individual's concrete experience that caused it. Probably it would spread by word of mouth by being adopted into the common way of speaking. Only then would it be written down, either as part of a narrative or in a deliberate gathering together of wisdom sayings.

Thus, it is highly unlikely that the title "The proverbs of Solomon" is meant to suggest that Solomon was responsible for the whole process by which all the included sayings reached their present written form. It is more likely that he took it upon himself to gather as much of the oral wisdom tradition that he could and to commit it to writing. To this he would have added some sayings based on his own experiences. It may be that Solomon was concerned to promote the pursuit of wisdom in Israel, recognising that his reign in a time of peace and unmatched prosperity was ideally suited to reflection on the nature of God's kingdom. It would be wrong to see this work as the activity of one of the idle rich. Wisdom is concerned with the details of life as they relate to the sense of a goal and purpose in human existence. Solomon was no dilettante amusing himself in a new form of literary activity, but a creative theologian anxious to show that life could be lived in a meaningful and fulfilling way within the framework of the covenant.

The shape of the book and the problem of how to use it

On first sight the book of Proverbs appears to be the result of accident rather than of careful planning. There are at least eight clearly distinguishable sections, each with its own characteristics, but there appears to be little order within each section and the composition of the book lacks any obvious logic. One is tempted to see it as an anthology or unplanned collection of documents that are themselves lacking in design. Various attempts have been made to see some kind of deliberate design in the way the book is put together, but without much agreement.

If, however, we let the book speak for itself there is little doubt that the final organiser or editor had a definite purpose in mind. The prologue (1:1-7) indicates that there is a clear intention to promote wisdom and understanding among various groups of people. It is very unlikely that the compiler would announce such an important goal without doing some hard thinking about how to organise the material. The structure may not be obvious to us at first, but on that basis we must not suggest that there is none.

The sections of the book are:

1. The prologue and stated purpose (1:1-7);
2. Various instructions (1:8-9:18);
3. The proverbs of Solomon (10:1-22:16);
4. More instructions (22:17-24:34);
5. The proverbs of Solomon copied by Hezekiah's men (25:1-29:27);
6. The words of Agur (30:1-33);
7. The words of Lemuel (31:1-9);
8. The praise of a good wife (31:10-31).

Scholarly debate about the structure of the book will no doubt continue. For the purposes of a non-technical book such as this, we must be content to note that the editor of Proverbs regards it as a course of instruction with a definite purpose. Our concern is to understand as best we can how to use the book in a way that enables it to fulfil its purpose in our lives.

Wisdom is not law.

I suppose one of the most common misunderstandings about Proverbs is its relationship to the law of Israel. A fairly popular approach is to see the proverbial sayings and the instructions as examples of the applications of the precepts of the law to daily life. Now, there is no doubt that we cannot completely separate wisdom from the law, but we need to be aware of the dangers of simply regarding Proverbs as the "small print" to the Sinai law. The following diagram is intended to represent the relation of the three main aspects of wisdom that are open to us. These are the concern of Proverbs, while the secret wisdom of God is reflected on in Job.

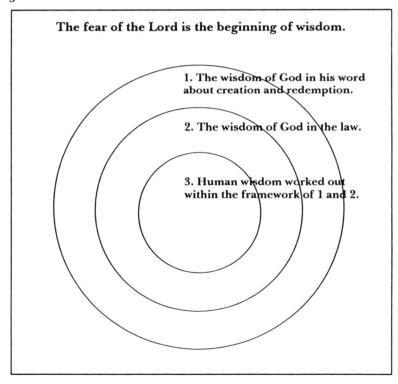

The fear of the Lord is the beginning of wisdom.

1. The wisdom of God in his word about creation and redemption.

2. The wisdom of God in the law.

3. Human wisdom worked out within the framework of 1 and 2.

Bearing in mind what I have said about the wisdom of God and the wisdom task given to the human race, it should help us to clarify the relationship of law and wisdom. At the risk of oversimplifying the matter, we should begin by thinking of the law as a principle element of the revealed word of God. We must not forget that the law was given within the framework of the revelation of God's grace in saving his people.

Now think of grace (redemption), law and human wisdom as three concentric circles. The outer circle that encompasses all else is the revealed wisdom of God that is the truth about creation and redemption. In New Testament terms this is the gospel, for it is specifically referred to as the wisdom of God (see 1 Cor 1:18-31). Within the framework of the wisdom of God in the grace of redemption, God gave the law to instruct his people in certain matters of life that was to be lived consistently with the grace that saved them. Thus the law is dependent for its meaning on the redemptive grace of God. Finally we see the human task of wisdom inside the framework of grace and law. Yet it is not simply an application of the revealed law in the details of life; it takes in all of human experience whether or not the law speaks directly to it. There is much in daily life for which there is no clear prescript of the law. God never intended that we should operate at the level of legalists who are driven only by instructions from above. He made us to be responsible, thinking, reasoning people who consider matters before us and make choices. Responsible freedom within the bounds set by God's word is very close to the heart of the human wisdom of Proverbs.

In the Old Testament, and particularly in the book of Deuteronomy, "the fear of the Lord" means conformity to the revealed word of God. It is reverent obedience to the law. Obedience to the law only exists as a response to the grace of God in redemption. For Israel there was an outward keeping of the law that had to be accompanied by obedience from the heart. Thus the trusting obedience towards the will of God was seen as a circumcision of the heart (Dt 10:14-16). The heart is only circumcised when there is faith in the God who redeems by grace. Any other kind of obedience is outward and self-justifying. The fear of the Lord is the beginning, the outer framework, within which knowledge and wisdom proceed (Prov 1:7).

In practical terms, then, the wisdom of Proverbs may operate at any of the three levels mentioned above. It may refer to the grace of God in redemption. It may refer to the law either in some particular detail or in general. Furthermore, and this is the largest part of wisdom, it may reflect on any of a multitude of experiences or concerns that are part of our common human lot.

Understanding the different forms within Proverbs

There are a number of different literary forms in Proverbs which function in distinct ways in conveying wisdom. Understanding literary forms and how they work is vital to understanding the Bible as a whole. This is not a difficult matter once we recognise that we all choose different ways of saying or writing things. We look for an acceptable way of saying something so that it will be recognised and clearly understood by our hearers or readers. For example, an advertising leaflet for a new shop opening in the district will be different in form from a union representative's report on the working conditions of employees in that same shop. Writing an application for a job in a retail company will be different from a letter written to the same company complaining about poor service. We can learn a lot about the intention of writers from the way they form or present their material. So, in the Bible a precept of the law of Moses has a different appearance and a different function from a psalm of praise, a historical narrative or a proverb. When we look at the book of Proverbs we find several different forms of literature that each seem to function in distinct ways. The most prominent forms are the *single-sentence proverbs*, the *instructions* and the *numerical sayings*.

The form of the single-sentence proverb is a study in itself and we must content ourselves here with its main aspects. The most obvious characteristic is what is called *parallelism*. Essentially, this describes the way a sentence is divided into two parts, and the way the second part contrasts, develops or complements the first:

A wise son brings joy to his father,
but a foolish son grief to his mother. (10:1)

The second line states the opposite (or antithesis) of the first in what is called *antithetic parallelism*. The contrast is sometimes stated in relative terms; that is, instead of opposing good to bad it says one is better than the other:

Better a little with the fear of the Lord
than great wealth with turmoil. (15:16)

Stating the same thing in two ways, usually with some slight variation in meaning, produces *synonymous parallelism*:

A man lacking in judgment strikes hands in pledge
and puts up security for his neighbour. (17:18).

When the one idea of the first line is developed in the second we have a synthesis of two sayings or *synthetic parallelism*:

The labourer's appetite works for him;
his hunger drives him on. (16:26)

These forms may be varied in lots of ways, but the examples help us to approach the text of Proverbs with a readiness to see how the sentence wisdom functions.

There are other aspects of the sentences which need some comment. Remember that often the Hebrew way of writing things is very different from the way we use English. This poses certain problems for the translators of the text and these show up in our English Bibles. Two examples may be given here. First, Hebrew has a little word that, depending on the context can be translated several ways. This is the word that does the job of our English word "and." In Hebrew, it can mean several other things such as "but," and "or," and some similar words used to connect two phrases. The translators must decide the best English equivalent in each case.

There is, however, another translation problem that has more important consequences than the one just mentioned. Sometimes the Hebrew provides no word and most of the English translators have inserted one. We find this, for example, in 25:11-14, 18, 19 and 26. The first of these verses is translated as:

A word aptly spoken
is like apples of gold in settings of silver. (25:11)

The Hebrew contains no word for "is like." It simply places the two ideas side by side without any indication that the second is the basis of a value judgment about the first. Thus, it seems, that one way of dealing with experiences in order to gain wisdom was simply to group things without stating explicitly the basis for the grouping. It served as a kind of exercise in abstraction that had the effect of training the readers to look beneath the surface for relationships and order.

Another way of doing this is seen in the numerical saying. It seems that the intention here is to put like with like, but not to try to specify what makes them alike (e.g. 6:16-19). Proverbs is concerned with the orderliness of life and the universe despite all contrary appearances. It is quite possible that we have here a technique for helping us to find relationships where none at first sight exist.

Perhaps the most obvious feature of much of the proverbial sentence literature is the contrasting of the two ways to live. This is put variously in terms of wisdom against folly, wickedness against righteousness and other contrasts of the good and acceptable life with that which leads to destruction. Examples are:

The righteous man is rescued from trouble,
and it comes on the wicked instead. (11:8)

A fool finds pleasure in evil conduct,
but a man of understanding delights in wisdom. (10:23)

The second main form in Proverbs is the longer instructional word. This has the flavour of the schoolroom or, at least, of regular teaching in the home. It is usually to be recognised by an introductory call to the son (or perhaps a pupil) to listen or pay attention. Several exhortations are accompanied by statements about why this teaching is sound and what will result if it is followed:

Listen, my son, to your father's instruction
and do not forsake your mother's teaching.
They will be a garland to grace your head
and a chain to adorn your neck.
My son, if sinners entice you,
do not give in to them.
If they say, "Come along with us;

> *let's lie in wait for someone's blood,*
> *let's waylay some harmless soul . .."* -
> *my son, do not go along with them,*
> *do not set foot on their paths;*
> *for their feet rush into sin,*
> *they are swift to shed bloo*d. (1:8-11, 15-16)

Some have assumed that these longer instructions represent a later and more theological type of wisdom than the proverbial sentences. There is, however, no convincing evidence of this. Similar instruction forms are to be found in Egyptian wisdom literature alongside proverbial sentences. It is better that we consider different forms and content for their purpose and function, and for the social context from which they emerged.

The numerical saying has a characteristic form in Proverbs that is similar to that found in the oracles of the prophet Amos against the nations (Amos 1-2). Biblical scholars offer various explanations for this form which follows a formula of numbers: n, n+1. Thus Amos says, "For three (n) sins of Damascus, even for four (n+1), I will not turn back my wrath" (Amos 1:3). Note the following examples from Proverbs:

> *There are three things that are too amazing for me,*
> *four that I do not understand:* (30:18)

> *Under three things the earth trembles,*
> *under four it cannot bear up:* (30:21)

It is possible that these sayings in wisdom fit into the process of classification. In this case the commonly used format of "three" followed by "four" would indicated an assembly of items that have some common feature. There may even be a kind of open-endedness that invites the student of wisdom to add further items. Again there is the underlying assumption that order and relationships have to be sought out.

Other wisdom literary forms exist which do not immediately concern us since they are not found in Proverbs.

Is there a theology of wisdom?

During the earlier part of the twentieth century, there was renewed interest in the study of the wisdom literature of the Bible. There was also much activity in the study of biblical theology. Biblical theology, contrary to what some might expect, is not merely the study of theology that comes from the Bible, but a study of theology in the way it unfolds in the Bible. Biblical theology looks at the process of revelation throughout redemptive history. In terms of wisdom literature, biblical theologians demanded an answer to the question of what theology was to be found there.

It is obvious that one of the most prominent features of the Old Testament is the way it portrayed the history of Israel as that in which God reveals himself by his activity of redeeming his people. The recognition of Old Testament history as the history of redemption was widely accepted. The problem with the wisdom literature was that it seemed almost totally unaware of the great redemptive historical events such as the covenant, the exodus, Sinai, and the whole priestly and prophetic ministry within Israel. Indeed, much of the material in Proverbs has no "God-talk" at all. It began to seem as if Proverbs, Job and Ecclesiastes had a very different perspective on God and human existence from that contained in the rest of the Old Testament.

It was never seriously suggested that the wise men and women of Israel had a different religion from the rest of the people; they must have believed the covenant promises of God and been attentive to the law of Moses. But why, then, did they make almost no reference to these things in their wisdom writings?

Let us return to some matters that I outlined in the first three chapters of this book. The first thing to remember is that Proverbs has been given, probably by the final editor, an introduction that states its basic theological perspective: "The fear of the Lord is the beginning of knowledge" (1:7). In Exodus 6:2-6 we are reminded that the Hebrew name *Yahweh*, from which the English form "Jehovah" is derived, is the personal name of God. It is linked to his revelation of himself as the God of the covenant of redemption. English translations have followed the ancient Jewish custom of avoiding the use of the holy name of God and of substituting the word "Lord." Proverbs 1:7 (and 9:10) thus acknowledges that all true wisdom and knowledge starts with the proper response of reverence and trust in the God of the covenant. This is the main assumption behind the biblical idea of the human task of gaining knowledge and learning wisdom.

The second thing to note is that Proverbs reminds us that godly thought and action do not have to be continually pinned down with "God-talk." It serves as a rebuke to the artificial piety which feels that the Lord must be referred to in every second phrase we utter. Not only is this not necessary, but it can actually distort reality in a very serious way. God made us in his image and, within the initial framework of his word, gave us freedom to pursue life with responsible freedom. Adam and Eve broke the bounds of that freedom with catastrophic effects. Now, the redemptive love of God is restoring to true humanity all who accept his grace in Jesus Christ. Wisdom, particularly in Proverbs, reminds us that being human means making human decisions for human acts and then wearing the consequences. The Bible knows nothing of the kind of piety once expressed to me by a sincere but rather mistaken Christian who said, "Isn't it great that we don't have to make any decisions." The person who expresses every human event as the Lord's doing debases what it means for us to be humans created in God's image. The Christian who thinks that the height of dedication and holiness is to let Jesus live his life through us is not only unrealistic but quite unbiblical.

This latter consideration has led some scholars to consider the wisdom literature as emphasising the theology of creation rather than redemption. This is a helpful suggestion provided we don't make the mistake of separating and even opposing creation and redemption as if they were irreconcilable perspectives. When we recognise that redemption is the work of God by which he is restoring the whole of creation to its intended order, there can be no separation. Furthermore, the original creation has practical relevance to us now only because it is being restored by redemption. Perhaps it is more productive to think of the theological orientation of Proverbs as that of how human beings, created in the image of God, are intended by God to function in the world.

Wisdom and world views

Christianity involves a total view of reality. The gospel is relevant to everything because God made everything. In meeting the challenges of the modern secular world, Christians need to understand not only their own foundational beliefs but also those of the non-Christian; too often we find ourselves arguing the case at the level of people's perceived problems or objections to the Christian view. We believe that the world is created by a sovereign and personal God who communicates with us by his word. The unbeliever rarely tackles us at this level of our basic assumptions. The argument is more likely to be over some technical question that is seen to contradict Christian belief.

The non-Christian also tends to write faith off because it deals with things that cannot be proved scientifically. When we meet this kind of objection we need to recognise that it is a clash of assumptions. The empiricist ("seeing is believing") should not be allowed to get away with the unquestioned assumption that it is more reasonable or logical to hold such a view. The idea that only the observable is real is itself only an assumption.

Apologetics is the name given to the business of rationally arguing the case for Christianity. While we know full well that only the gospel will finally convert a person, we may need to help the unbeliever clear away a lot of prejudices to faith before he or she is willing to listen to the gospel. To achieve this we have to do two things: show the reasonableness of Christian assumptions and show the inner contradictions of non-Christian assumptions. The Christian world view must be clearly understood and fearlessly defended.

Proverbs and the rest of the biblical wisdom literature can help us in this task. One aspect of apologetics is recognising what we understand about our minds and the way we gain knowledge. Proverbs is especially helpful here because it blends two important aspects of gaining knowledge in a particular way. It recognises the validity of the use of all our faculties to observe and to reason about the nature of reality. In this it is empirical or, if you like, scientific. It also understands our sinful human nature as that which needs redemptive revelation from God.

The authentically Christian world view is based upon the revelation of God which is in Jesus Christ and in all the Old Testament revelation as that which foreshadows him. It also involves empirical or scientific knowledge gathered and interpreted in the light of God's revelation. Perhaps we need to stress that the statement "the fear of the Lord is the beginning of knowledge" is all inclusive; a true response to God is the only basis for a true understanding of all reality. The assumptions of Christianity are reasonable and explain our experience of reality better that all other assumptions.

Unlike the assumptions of secular thinking, Christian assumptions are sustainable because they do not contradict themselves.

Though much of Proverbs appears to be secular in tone it nevertheless challenges secular world views. While being immensely practical, it is based on a theory of knowledge that takes prior account of what God says in his word. The common ground between Israel's wisdom and that of pagans does not permit us to walk with pagans in partial agreement with their view of ultimate reality. Proverbs shows rather that we must challenge every attempt to evaluate what is right and true, what is wise and good, which does not submit to the fear of the Lord.

5

Instructions
Proverbs 1:1-9:18

Selected unit - Proverbs 1:1-7

Description

The editor of Proverbs has set out to be "user friendly."
He has designed the structure of the whole book with a
definite purpose that he wants the reader to know about right
from the start. This little prologue is important in showing
us that Proverbs has an educational purpose, in the general
sense, of teaching people a particular kind of skill in life.
Essentially it is the skill of wisdom or right understanding,
and of what makes for the good life.

The theme of Proverbs and its basic perspective on reality
is summed up in 1:7 as "the fear of the Lord." The practical
nature of so much of this book reminds us that Hebrew
wisdom was utterly comprehensive. No area of human
knowledge lay outside the dimension that is governed by a
right relationship to the living God who had revealed himself
in the great saving events within Israel's history.

Text

1:1 The book is a collection of wisdom after the style of Solomon (see chapter 4 above, "By whom and when?"). As the designated patron of Israel's wisdom movement, Solomon not only probably wrote much that is in this collection, but he also lent the authority of his name to this approach of gaining knowledge. The word "proverb" has become a technical term applied mostly to the single-sentence sayings found in chapters 10 and following, but here it is given more general application to all kinds of wisdom sayings.

1:2 *wisdom.* A word that is often used as a synonym for knowledge. In verses 2-6, a series of alternate words helps to pin down its elusive meaning. The explicit purpose indicated for the book suggests some kind of formal education was in mind, whether in a school or at home. *discipline.* Ordered thinking leading to right actions. *insight.* the ability to see what is not openly obvious in meanings and relationships.

1:3 *prudent life.* Defined by the following phrase. *right and just and fair.* Although capable of a purely worldly meaning, these words are all at the centre of the Israelite's perspective on the character of God as it defines relationships.

1:4 *prudence.* A different Hebrew word from that in verse 3. It refers to shrewdness of thinking. *simple.* Not a low I.Q. but a lack of experience in life which leaves one vulnerable. *discretion.* The ability to make the right decision.

1:5 This book can also be used in "graduate" studies; there is always more that can by learned about life by reflecting on and applying the principles that are to be found here.

1:6 *for understanding proverbs and parables . . and riddles*: probably distinct forms of wisdom sayings but the distinctions have become blurred or obscured. More important than being able to identify exactly how these terms were originally used is recognising the variety of forms in use in Proverbs. Again the purpose of the book is stated. The implication is that the form and content of the whole collection is sufficient to fulfil this purpose since there is no discourse on the nature of wisdom literary forms and how they function.

1:7 *The fear of the Lord*. This "fear" must be distinguished from any idea of terror. It is a phrase used constantly throughout Scripture to describe the appropriate response of human beings to the self-revelation of the God who has created and redeemed his people (similar phrases are found in 2:4-6; 9:10; 15:33; Ps 111:10; Job 28:28). Thus, it carries the notion of reverent awe and submissive faith. It is also important to note that it is not some vague response to an idea of deity, but an encounter with the Lord God of Israel. We truly respond to him only when we respond to what he reveals about himself and about his purposes for his creation. (See chapter 4: Is there a theology of wisdom?) The reference to God as "Lord" means the God of the covenant and the redeeming God. This places Proverbs squarely within the covenant faith of Israel. *is the beginning of knowledge*. The "beginning" can mean both the starting point and the chief goal or principle. What God reveals in his word is the only real basis for understanding what life is about. The significance of this is highlighted by the typical use of antithetic parallelism in the second line of this verse.

Function

This section acts as a distinctive prologue to the whole book. It makes an authority claim by aligning the work with Solomon, and describes the goals of this course in wisdom. Because such wisdom, even in the forms found here, has common ground with pagan or merely human wisdom, the essential difference is given in verse 7. This is a summons to undertake the quest for wisdom only within the framework of God's revelation of his covenant commitment to Israel. It recognises that Israel's God is the only God, that he is the creator of all things and therefore gives all things their meaning and purpose. It also understands that everything in all creation is caught up in God's purposes of redemption for his people.

Testimony to Christ

Solomon was the prime mover of the Israelite wisdom movement that continued into the New Testament where its chief exponent is Jesus. The significance of Solomon as the son of David is given theological weight in many places in Scripture. He was to be the representative son of God and the son of David (2 Sam 7:14). This means that he is seen at the centre of God's purposes to save his people. The theme of the Davidic prince is prominent in the prophets and psalms, and is on occasions linked with the true wisdom that is from God (e.g. Isa 9:6-7; 11:1-5). Isaiah refers to the messianic prince from the dynasty of David and says of him:

> *The Spirit of the Lord will rest on him -*
> *the Spirit of wisdom and of understanding,*
> *the Spirit of counsel and of power,*
> *the Spirit of knowledge and of the fear of the Lord -*
> *and he will delight in the fear of the Lord.* (Isa 11:2-3a)

When Jesus the Son of David comes, he shows he is the most able wisdom teacher of all, and that he is not merely a wise man but the source of wisdom (see Mt 7:24-27). He is the one who is greater than Solomon and who has come with the greatest wisdom from God (see Lk 11:29-32, 52). Jesus, the God-man, is the source of divine wisdom and also the representative man of God, the true Israelite, and thus the one who expresses perfect human wisdom on our behalf.

Israel's wisdom showed that the whole of life needed to be integrated within the revelation of God's word. The gospel brings this dimension to fullness as we find that the saving work of Jesus is about the restoration of our humanity in him. It is about the redemption of the created order from its bondage to futility and decay due to human sin (Rom 8:19-21). As Christians we have the same kind of wisdom task that the ancient Israelite had. We must learn to live in a fallen world that is in the process of being redeemed, and we must learn what makes for the good, productive, God-honouring life. The most important distinction between us and the Israelites is not the development in human culture, scientific knowledge and technology. It is the fact that we can now see the greatest revelation of God's wisdom in Jesus Christ. We have a distinct advantage in knowing the fear of the Lord, for we can respond to the Christ of the gospel and learn to understand reality in the light of his life, death and resurrection.

Questions

1. What do you know of Solomon's place in the wisdom tradition of Israel? Read 1 Kings 1 to 10 and note the breadth of meaning given to Solomon's wisdom.

2. What kind of agenda for learning wisdom does this section set?

3. What is meant by "the fear of the Lord," and in what sense is it the beginning of knowledge?

Comments on Proverbs 1:8-19

This section is in the form of "instruction" (see chapter 4 above, "Understanding the different forms within Proverbs"). It begins with the teacher's call to the pupil to pay attention to the teaching. Here the tutorial takes place in the home and both father and mother are involved.

1:8 *instruction . . . teaching.* Synonyms. Both terms indicate more than mere information giving; rather, the imparting of knowledge that is life- or character-shaping.

1:9 Wisdom beautifies the life of the diligent student.

1:10-19 Possibly a new unit, or it may continue the previous two verses by giving specific content to the instruction. The authority of true wisdom is seen in the commands that are typical of the instruction form (vv. 10b, 15).

1:11 *lie in wait.* Folly is not mere ignorance or inexperience. Here it is to pursue actively a course of evil. Though wisdom is not to be reduced to morality, the moral dimension is still there.

1:12 *the grave* (Hebrew: *sheol*). The place of the departed. Here it is used as a metaphor of being completely overwhelmed.

1:13 *valuable things.* It is not wealth as such that is condemned but the use of evil to get it. Wisdom recognises the legitimate place of material wealth (e.g. in Solomon's kingdom) but shows that there is greater wealth to be had in wisdom itself (e.g. 2:4; 3:13-16; Job 28:12-19).

1:16 See Romans 3:15.

1:17-18 This proverbial saying seems to have been introduced to give extra force to the motive.

1:19 Proverbs presupposes an orderliness in the universe that is born out in the bulk of experience. Those who live foolishly will come to a sticky end. Sometimes experience contradicts this and we have the problem of why the righteous suffer (e.g. Job) while the wicked prosper (e.g. Ps 73).

Selected unit - Proverbs 1:20-33

Description

The author of this section uses a powerful poetic technique to convey the nature of wisdom. He portrays wisdom as a woman engaged in a kind of evangelism, calling any who will hear to receive what she has to offer. There is urgency in the warning that highlights the place of true wisdom in life. "Simple ones," "mockers" and "fools" all need to repent of their rejection of wisdom before retribution overtakes them. There is a very strong acceptance of the natural working of retribution here and in the whole of Proverbs. The focus is not on the judgment of God so much as on the created order of things, so that to ignore or to defy it is to invite disaster. Those who deliberately reject wisdom will find that it becomes harder and harder to arrest the downward slide to destruction. Nevertheless, wisdom will always be there for those who truly seek her.

Text

1:20 The open-air preacher is similar to the prophet in Isaiah 55:1-2. Personification of wisdom is also found in 3:14-18; 8:1-36; 9:1-12. It is purely poetic and not an attempt to invest wisdom with any semi-divine existence.

1:21 *gateways.* A reflection of Israelite social custom. The town gate was the traditional gathering place where matters of justice and public interest were dealt with.

1:22 *simple ones.* See verse 4 and note. Now there is a development in that the simple must make a deliberate choice between the two ways of wisdom and folly, of righteousness and wickedness. Proverbs constantly presents this choice and thus shows the moral dimension of wisdom.

1:23 *I would have poured out my heart.* Wisdom is both the human task and the gift of God. The gift comes first in the gracious revelation of God to us. The human task is to respond to what God says about our humanness. As we do so, we find that God responds to our response by increasing our wisdom.

1:24 *you rejected me.* A similar rejection is reflected in Psalm 78 where Israel is shown to play the fool by refusing the grace of God in his saving acts. The psalm is introduced as a wisdom instruction (Ps 78:1-2).

1:27 The disaster is not wisdom's doing but the inevitable outcome of folly. It is not seen here as divine intervention but as that which is built into the order of the universe.

1:28 *I will not answer.* As with the grace of God in salvation there comes a decisive point when rejection continues.

Presumption on the forbearance of the giver is ruled out. Since life is a gift it is the height of folly to reject it and still expect it to be offered.

1:29 *to fear the Lord*. See note on verse 7. This reminds us that wisdom is not being portrayed as some independent being or entity. The human task of gaining wisdom will not be successful if redemptive revelation is rejected.

1:31 *fruit*. The normal consequences of folly will be like the results of gluttony.

1:32 *waywardness*. The "simple" here are more than merely immature (see v. 4) in that they are indifferent to wisdom. *complacency*. These "fools" are quite sure that they have no need to learn from anyone.

1:33 *whoever listens to me*. That is, takes in and acts upon the instructions. *will live in safety*. The normal expectation in Proverbs is that a wise life avoids the perils that can threaten existence. Eternity is not in view here. *and be at ease*. "The fear of the Lord" (see v. 7) involves trust in the loving care of God who watches over his people. However, there is also the sense that wisdom enables us to take a measure of control over our lives so that we avoid harmful situations.

Function

The call of wisdom is presented here in such a way as to show that the refusal to seek true wisdom through the fear of the Lord is both blameworthy and destructive. Old Testament wisdom frequently causes us to focus on the significance of the role of God as creator. In effect it is saying God made everything, including us, and God alone can define the purpose and meaning of everything. If he made us to know him and to submit to his rule, then to live in any other way is corrupt and rebellious. Life is an inestimable gift that is defined by God's purposes and our relationship to him. There is a total rejection here of any notion that we are neutral in the matter, or that the values in life can be properly assessed by the independent human mind.

Testimony to Christ

The general question in Old Testament wisdom is how should an Israelite live responsibly before God. The wisdom "gospel" in this passage involves both the gift of wisdom, and the call to receive it. It warns against refusing the offered gift since it is the only way to secure life. But the act of receiving wisdom's gift implies the human task of searching for knowledge.

As Christians seeking to apply this passage without distorting it or turning it into an exercise of the imagination, we must first ask how it functions in its own context as a revelation of God's ways with people. Then we try to identify the same function in our theological context in the gospel. Behind the warning is the self-giving of wisdom to all who will receive her. Christ, as we have seen, is the wisdom of God and gives himself to whoever will receive him; the gospel can never be reduced to a vague or warm experience.

Christ as the gift fulfils two aspects of wisdom. He is the self-revelation of God by which alone we can know life. To put it another way, the person and work of Christ are the foundational wisdom for life (see 1 Cor 1:23-30). He is also the true and wise Israelite who fulfils for us the purpose of God for his people. Jesus, as a boy at the temple with the teachers of the law and as the young man growing in wisdom (see Lk 2:41-52), has fulfilled on our behalf the human role of fearing the Lord and being wise for life's tasks. When we fail to act as wisely as we should, we, who have received Christ, can know that the failure is covered by the merits of Christ who is the perfectly wise human for us.

Questions

1. How is wisdom portrayed here?

2. What two things are contrasted in the passage?

3. What are the main results of refusing wisdom, and of receiving it?

4. In what sense is wisdom something given to us and in what sense something we have to achieve?

5. How does the gift of wisdom relate to our position as Christians? What is the wisdom which is given to us (read 1 Cor 1-2)?

Comments on Proverbs 2:1-31

This chapter is a typical instruction, beginning with the address followed by a series of conditional "if" and consequential "then" clauses. The commonly used command (see 1:8, 10, 15; 3:1) is not found here. The strength of the appeal lies in the power of wisdom to deliver us from death. The two aspects of wisdom as gift and task are clearly seen (e.g. vv. 4, 6).

2:2 *turning your ear*. Paying careful attention. *heart*. To the Hebrews, the seat of the reason and will; not the centre of emotion as in Western thought. Formal or outward acceptance of wisdom is ruled out; there must be true assent of the will coupled with compliance.

2:3 Wisdom is a gift of God that is there for the asking.

2:4 Wisdom is also the human task that wisdom from God enables us to pursue.

2:5 *you will understand the fear of the Lord.* In 1:7 "the fear of the Lord" is the starting point for gaining wisdom, but here it is the goal. God gives the knowledge of himself in his redemptive revelation and, from this, the wise person engages in the task of learning more wisdom and of knowing God.

2:6 *the Lord gives wisdom.* Human experience in the search for wisdom is dependent on God who is the source of all truth. *from his mouth.* God communicates by his word, not by feeling or mystical impulse.

2:7 *victory.* "Sound wisdom" (RSV); that is, in the sense of a successful life. Here the condition is uprightness that is almost certainly synonymous with fearing the Lord.

2:8 *he guards . . . and protects.* There is a clear theological perspective here that is only implicit in 1:33. God not only builds a natural retribution into the order of things, he is actively watching over his people.

2:9 *every good path.* Guidance means that we have the wisdom to know the good paths from the bad ones. God does not make our decisions for us; rather he equips us with the wisdom to choose the course that is consistent with the goal to which he is bringing us.

2:10 *soul.* This word has a range of meanings in the Bible. Here it is probably a synonym for life.

2:12-15. The fools and perverse people of this world are actually attempting to overthrow the order that God has preserved despite the fallen condition of the world.

2:16 *adulteress*. Part of God's order is human relationships, including sexual behaviour. Adultery is a contradiction of the most intimate human relationship and is especially damaging to life (see 5:1-23; 6:20-29; 7:1-27). The Hebrew word here is literally "foreign, or strange, woman" and, in this context, means one who is foreign to the proper ideals of marriage.

2:17 *the covenant she made before God*. This could also be translated as "the covenant of her god" indicating perhaps a Canaanite who has left her husband for adultery or ritual prostitution. However, it is more likely that it refers to an Israelite adulteress who has broken the law of God. The NIV implies that the covenant refers to the marriage vows.

2:18 *death*. The opposite of the life that involves the right relationship with God. It is therefore an irreversible descent into the disorder of moral perversity.

2:20-22 The righteous wise possess true life that is here defined in the terms belonging to the covenant faith of Israel. The conditional aspect of the covenant is reflected here. The wise, or upright, inherit the land while the wicked are removed (see Ex 20:12; Dt 26:1-9; 28:1-24).

Selected unit - Proverbs 3:1-12

Description

This is another instruction addressed to the teacher's son or pupil. The address leads abruptly to the commands that are supported by motive clauses showing the blessings that follow from wisdom. Although the address is repeated in verse 11, it is probably a single literary unit. Verse 12 explains that the Lord's discipline is an expression of his love, thus making correction something to be welcomed. This passage does not specify any particular area of knowledge to be sought but rather exhorts the pupil to be constantly engaged in the pursuit of wisdom so that life may yield all of its riches.

Text

3:1 *teaching*. The Hebrew word is often translated "law." Its root meaning is instruction. Although wisdom may reflect the law it must be distinguished from it. There is an authority inherent to wisdom which demands acceptance. *commands*. In wisdom this word refers to counsel of the wise person and should not be read as referring to the commands of God in the law.

3:2 *prolong your life*. Proverbs emphasises the connection between wise behaviour and the achievement of a long and productive life. Such wisdom overlaps with the blessings expressed in the law (e.g. Ex 20:12), but is not regarded as the invariable case. *prosperity*. The Hebrew word used is *shalom* ("peace") and refers to harmony of relationships and wholeness, including health (see v. 8). This comes from the understanding of God's creation purposes and the recognition that his blessings are experienced in this physical world. In the Old Testament the idea of a totally new creation emerges only in the later prophets. Resurrection to the future life is an even later perspective in biblical revelation.

3:3 *love and faithfulness*. The Hebrew phrase *hesed v'emet* refers to the covenant and shows here that wisdom is understood in that framework. The authority of wisdom would lie in its being based on the truth revealed in God's covenant. *bind . . . neck.* A metaphor for the way wisdom beautifies one's life (cf. 1:9). *write . . . heart.* Commit to memory (as in v. 1).

3:4 *good name.* Literally "good success."

3:5 *Trust in the Lord.* See note on 1:7. The heart of wisdom is the fear of the Lord. *lean not on your own understanding.* A contrast between a perception of reality that takes God's revealed word as the starting point for all truth, and one that assumes that human understanding is the starting point.

3:6 *he will make your paths straight.* God's guidance lies in what he has revealed of his purposes for us in his saving acts and word. This is the framework within which we make decisions; there is no hint that guidance bypasses the human decision-making process.

3:7 *wise in your own eyes.* The humanistic assumption that our intellect and reason can assess all truth. *fear the Lord.* See note on 1:7.

3:8 See note on verse 2.

3:9 *Honour the Lord.* A synonym for fearing the Lord. *firstfruits.* The first part of the harvest that was given to the priests (see Lev 23:10; Num 18:12-13). One of the few references to the cultic requirements of the law in relation to wisdom.

3:10 True wisdom cannot ignore what God has revealed as his will, and thus keeping the law is a part of it. The wisdom perspective here is that God is involved in the natural order.

3:11 *discipline.* Usually a reference to education rather than chastisement, although the latter may come into it (cf. Heb 12:4-8 which suggests the hardship in discipline).

3:12 Discipline from God is loving and aimed at our ultimate good (see Heb 12:6).

Function

The form of the instruction is much more useful for theoretical discourses than is the shorter proverbial saying. In a manner similar to the prologue (1:1-7), this passage relates the two dimensions of wisdom. These are the gift of God's wisdom in his covenant revelation and the human task of gaining wisdom from experience. The practical issue of guidance is in view here. We are reminded of the human dimension that is not removed by faith or by the indwelling of God's Spirit. It is impossible in this context to take the promise of guidance away from the task of learning wisdom. There is no conflict between the idea that God makes our paths straight and the insistence on our task of learning to make decisions. Because it deals with the matter of learning wisdom in general rather than a specific area of experience, this passage reinforces the prologue's insistence on the priority of God's revelation. Thus, it functions as a useful preface to the collections of aphorisms or single-sentence wisdom sayings that come later in the book.

Testimony to Christ

Luke's comment on the boy Jesus in Luke 2:52 is almost certainly a reference to the wise pupil in Proverbs 3:4 (see comments on 1:20-33), though we do not need to borrow the reference to the son from verse 1 in order to see the relationship to Christ. Israel is also known as God's son (Ex

4:22-23; Hos 11:1), and the son of David was spoken of as the son of God who would represent all Israel in covenant relationship to God (see 2 Sam 7:14).

This wisdom passage in Proverbs 3 was at once practical and idealistic in its application. It set out the task for the student of wisdom but it was always beyond the ability of sinful people to fulfil perfectly. Solomon the temple builder was the son of David, the son of God, and wise man, although imperfectly.

Thus, Luke's thematic use of "son of God" referring to Jesus is instructive. The birth narrative in Luke is centred on the temple (note the role of the priest Zechariah in Lk 1:5-23) and the fulfilment of the covenant to Israel (e.g. Lk 1:72). It leads us to the birth of the true son of David who conforms to the law in his circumcision and purification at the temple, where Simeon identifies the infant Jesus as God's salvation (Lk 2:21-32). The narrative then jumps to the account of the twelve-year-old Jesus at the temple who "had to be in [his] Father's house" (Lk 2:49). Luke introduces the ministry of John the Baptist, and at his baptism Jesus is declared to be God's Son (Lk 3:22) when he fulfils righteousness for Israel (see Lk 1:67-75). It is this obedient and perfectly wise Son of God that Satan seeks to divert from his path (Lk 4:3), but Jesus has learned his wisdom too well from his Father and remains faithful.

Questions

1. How would you describe the literary form of an "instruction"? How does it function as a means of wisdom teaching?

2. What view of guidance is offered in this section?

3. What is the relationship between trusting the Lord and being disciplined by him?

4. How do verses 5 to 7 apply in the light of the gospel?

Comments on Proverbs 3:13-4:27

3:13-20 This section is formed more as a hymn in praise of wisdom than as a piece of instruction (cf. Ps 1).

3:13 *Blessed.* Sometimes translated "happy" but it is not a subjective feeling. Found almost exclusively in the Psalms and the wisdom writings, it refers to the good as God defines it.

3:14-15 See Job 28. One of the hardest lessons to learn is that some things are of far more value than material wealth.

3:16-17 See verse 2 and note.

3:18 *tree of life.* Probably not a reference to the tree in Eden (see Gen 2:9) though the author would have known of it. A tree is a natural metaphor for that which gives life (see also 11:30; 13:12; 15:4). Life is an important theme in Proverbs and is essentially relational. In Genesis 2:17 death stems from the disruption of the proper relationship with God who is the author of life. Because wisdom is concerned with the maintenance of proper relationships, it promotes life.

3:19-20 Wisdom literature makes few references to covenant and salvation, although, as we have seen in 1:7, it presupposes them. The good order established by God at creation was not totally destroyed by sin. Human wisdom consists in learning to understand the order that exists, while the wisdom of God is the source of the well-ordered creation (see also Prov 8:22-31).

3:21-26 Another instruction that deals with the theme of guidance in a general way.

3:22 *life*. See 1:33; 2:21; 3:2, 16-18 and notes.

3:23 *you will go on your way*. The making of wise decisions is the human side of guidance in daily life.

3:24 *you will not be afraid*. Life-threatening situations are the result of a disordered universe. While we may have to face danger in doing the will of God, the normal approach to life is to pursue right relationships and order.

3:25 *disaster . . . that overtakes the wicked*. The result of disorder as well as the direct judgment of God.

3:26 *the Lord will be your confidence*. The good order is not an independent entity; the Lord himself is active in the care of those who trust him.

3:27-35 This is a collection of negative precepts dealing with human relationships. The commands to avoid deceitfulness, planning evil against another, and contentiousness (vv. 28-31) appear to be supported by motive clauses in verses 32 to 35.

3:32 *the Lord detests*. In contrast to the common theme in Proverbs of the outworking of folly in natural retribution, the morality of these precepts is based on the character and will of the Lord. Such theologising is not characteristic of Proverbs.

3:33 *The Lord's curse.* The contrast between righteousness and wickedness is related to God's blessings and curses. This is similar to the emphasis in Deuteronomy in which faithfulness is rewarded by the blessings of God (see Dt 11:26-29; 28:1-19).

3:34-35 *gives grace to the humble.* These verses are also a reflection on wisdom as faithfulness to the revealed will of God in the covenant.

4:1-27 There are three instructional sayings in this chapter, each beginning with the usual address "my son" (vv. 1, 10, 20). The first recommends wisdom as the most precious acquisition, the second sees it as the path to life, and the third commends the way of uprightness. The absence of any reference to God or the covenant raises the question of the common human experience (see notes on 22:17-24:22 and the possible Egyptian connection). Solomon's exchange of wisdom with pagans (see 1 Ki 4:29-34; 10:1-9) shows that certain features of wisdom were shared across national and religious boundaries. Whenever the matter of common ground with pagan wisdom emerges it is important to remember the rule that Israel's wisdom was always within the framework of the revelation of God (see note on 1:7).

4:3 *tender.* Inexperienced in life. The importance of age and experience was recognised in Israelite society.

4:4 *live.* See notes on 2:18 and 3:2.

4:6 *Do not forsake . . . she will protect.* Wisdom invites trust and commitment and amply repays.

4:7 *Though it cost all.* Jesus uses a similar idea in his saying about the pearl of great price (see Mt 13:44-46). Gaining wisdom may mean forsaking temporal riches.

4:8-9 *exalt . . . honour . . . grace . . . splendour.* Wisdom always pays a good dividend.

4:10 *the years of your life will be many.* Wisdom promotes life. The Book of Job reminds us, however, that the wise person sometimes encounters what appear to be life-threatening situations in which the only recourse is to trust God.

4:11-12 *not be hampered.* Practical wisdom enables one to avoid the obstacles on the way to the goal of life.

4:13 *it is your life.* Meaning here that life cannot exist without wisdom. Later in biblical revelation there is a representative idea introduced that is related to the ministry of Jesus as our wisdom (see 1 Cor 1:30).

4:14 *the path of the wicked.* Wisdom, especially in the single-sentence sayings, typically makes contrasts between opposing ways and ideas. Wisdom and righteousness are set over and against folly and wickedness.

4:16 *they cannot sleep.* People become so addicted to evil that they will not sleep until they indulge in it.

4:17 *the bread of wickedness.* Wickedness becomes their staple diet.

4:18 *the path of the righteous . . . shining ever brighter.* Wisdom's righteousness is like the dawning of the day compared to the gloom of wickedness.

4:20-27 The implicit contrast here is between wisdom and folly. The wisdom teacher is not afraid to stress the mental effort needed to learn wisdom.

4:21 *heart.* The mind; see note on 2:2.

4:22 *health.* Wholeness and soundness; see 3:18 and note.

4:23 *the wellspring of life.* Literally "life goes out from it." The way we think is the way we act (see Mt 12:34-35; Mk 7:20-23; Rom 2:29; Jas 3:13-18).

4:24 *corrupt talk from your lips.* Words reflect what is in the heart.

4:25-27 An extended metaphor for life's way. Wisdom keeps one from going astray.

4:26 *only ways that are firm.* Pursue only wisdom.

4:27 *Do not swerve.* Persevere in gaining and applying the accumulated wisdom of the wise.

Selected unit - Proverbs 5:1-23

Description

This is another instruction (see comments on Prov 3:1-12 above, "Description"). It is conceivable that three separate units (vv. 1-6, 7-14, and 15-23) have been joined together here; the separate address to "sons" in verse 7 may indicate a second instruction, but not necessarily so.

The subject matter of the whole chapter provides a unity: sexual immorality is destructive of life, and sexual satisfaction should be found within the bond of marriage. The fact that chapters 5 and 7 along with part of chapter 6 are devoted to warnings against adultery shows how destructive it is. The graphic use of the instructional form and the dramatic narrative in 7:6-23 heightens the motivation to act wisely, and points to the insidious nature of sexual temptation.

Implicit in wisdom sayings and discourses is the contrast between wisdom and folly. The parallelism of the two-lined sentences is here matched by the contrast of sexual folly in verses 1 to 14 and the rewards of faithfulness to the marriage bond in verses 15 to 23.

Text

5:1-6 First there is the description of the adulteress. She presents as one who wants the best for her victim; it is only later that she is seen as she truly is: a destroyer of lives. It is quite likely that the woman is a prostitute rather than a married woman who strays into adultery.

5:2 *that . . . your lips may preserve knowledge.* Either to maintain a discreet silence, or to say something of consequence.

5:3 *her speech is smoother than oil.* Seduction begins with words that may sound wise and full of charm.

5:4 *but in the end.* The early promise is not realised and the result is the opposite to what was expected. *bitter as gall.* Gall is a plant with particularly bitter taste. It is used as a metaphor of bitter affliction (see Dt 29:18). *double-edged sword.* The promise of a relationship is not only empty but will actually bring injury.

5:5 *death.* Dissolute living may indeed cause an early death, however in this context it probably refers to the disordering of life so that it does not conform to life as defined by God. *grave.* In Hebrew, *sheol,* the place of the dead. If this is a metaphor here for the chaotic life, it is also the reality at which such a life eventually arrives.

5:6 *the way of life.* The way of wisdom which affirms ordered relationships. Sexual relationships that are not based on the marriage bond involve both parties treating each other as mere objects of physical gratification. *her paths are crooked.* Folly and wickedness, in whatever form, mean a rejection of God's order and plan.

5:7-14 The emphasis now switches to the terrible price of immorality.

5:8 *a path far from her.* The wise course is to make a conscious decision to keep out of the way of temptation by avoiding contact with the prostitute.

5:9-11 The young man who foolishly engages in immorality will find it exacts a high price.

5:9 *one who is cruel.* It may refer to the outraged husband of the adulterer, but more likely to the life-draining relationship itself.

5:10 *strangers feast on your wealth.* The dissipation of life and resources is the inevitable outcome of immorality.

5:11-14 *At the end of your life you will groan.* Such folly can only bring a deep sense of regret and sorrow in old age when one reflects on the squandering of life and reputation for the sake of brief moments of pleasure. The classic statement of regret is, "If only I had heeded the advice of wise teachers."

5:14 *in the midst of the whole assembly.* Either public disgrace, or the disapproval of the community of faith who applied the sanctions of the law.

5:15 *Drink water from your own cistern.* A metaphor for sexual relations. That is, find satisfaction from your own wife.

5:16-17 The Hebrew does not make clear if this is a question or a statement. The context suggests the former, referring to the wastefulness of promiscuity. There are a number of metaphors here which make exact interpretation difficult. The wife in verse 15 is referred to as a cistern. Then in verse 16 "springs" and "streams" appear to mean the husband's sexual powers which should not be wasted on strangers.

5:18 *fountain.* Probably a metaphor for the wife as the bearer of children.

5:19 *a graceful doe.* The imagery of a graceful animal of rare beauty emphasises physical pleasures as integral to sexual relations however these may be hedged by the law or by the perceptible order of things. The erotic language used here approaches that of the Song of Songs (see Song 1:2-3; 4:1-7).

5:21-23 *a man's ways are in full view of the Lord.* It is possible that these verses have been added to give a more directly theological thrust to the whole passage. Warnings against the natural consequences of sexual folly are also found in non-Israelite wisdom. The revelation of God reminds us that ultimately it is the judgment of God that we face when we reject his good order and purpose for humanity. The passage does not suggest that God brings immediate retribution on every sin. Rather he oversees the retributive order in creation so that a person's folly will ensnare him or her. This matter still has the perspective of wisdom rather than law: a reason for what the law says in a prescriptive ordinance (e.g. Ex 20:14) is perceptible in the experiences that wisdom reflects on and learns from.

Function

The passage functions as a warning against the perils of sexual immorality. While this unit, as wisdom literature, is unusually oriented to the covenant, we must recognise also the wisdom perspective on the orderliness of the universe. Wisdom struggles to come to terms with the effects of sin or folly both in its original effect of bringing disorder into reality, and in its continuous disruption of the order that has been preserved by the goodness and wisdom of God. It is the fact that the latter can be perceived in its destructive effects on human existence that gives this wisdom a universal appeal even to those who reject the special revelation of God. It is a demonstrable fact, to those who will see, that monogamous and permanent marriage relationships are the proper context for sexual relationships. There is much else that can go wrong in a marriage, but even pagans can recognise that the fabric of human society depends upon the maintenance of sexual ethics.

Testimony to Christ

Wisdom's reflections carry much implicit thinking about what humanity was intended to be and how people were meant to function in their personal and sexual relationships. The whole notion of folly or unrighteousness stands against the background of the sin of Adam and Eve and consequent "fall" of the entire created order. As wisdom speaks out of the still preserved order and in the framework of the revelation of God in the covenant, it presupposes a true Adam, a righteous and wise humankind. As it speaks out of the covenant to Israel, it presupposes a true Israel, a righteous and wise people of God.

It is important to recognise that the Christian application of such a passage, and indeed of any biblical passage, must follow a pathway through Christ who fulfils the intention of God for Adam and for Israel. This is the only path that will save us from frustrating legalism in attempting to make the passage relevant to us now.

Here we see the most intimate of all human relationships with its potential for good and evil. Although Jesus was not married he was a truly human person and therefore a sexual being. He expressed his sexuality perfectly in his relationships with others, and he also taught much concerning human relationships to show the true foundation of them. By living a perfect human life on our behalf he fulfilled all that God intended for Adam and for Israel. He thus justified our human relationships, and our failure to be what we should be is forgiven if we are united to him by faith. This is part of what it means for Christ to be our wisdom (see 1 Cor 1:30).

Once we have pinned the teaching of the Old Testament into its fulfilment in Christ then its application to us follows in the same way that all ethical exhortation in the New Testament is applied. In Christ we are justified and forgiven for our failures. We are also raised to a new life in Christ so that what he was for us in his human perfection becomes the goal towards which we now strive day by day.

Questions

1. What is the teaching of this passage on sexual ethics?

2. Why is sexual immorality seen to be so destructive?

3. In what sense do verses 15 to 23 present a Christian sexual morality?

Comments on Proverbs 6:1-8:21

6:1-5 This first unit is an instruction warning against entering an unwise agreement of surety. It is not prudent to bind yourself to an agreement that results in your having to take the responsibility for another's foolishness.

6:1 *struck hands in pledge.* A custom similar to shaking hands on a deal.

6:2 *trapped by what you said.* Rashly agreeing to go surety for another and so to walking into a trap of one's own making.

6:3 *fallen into your neighbour's hands.* By accepting responsibility for another's debts you allow him or her to take control of your life.

6:4 *Allow no sleep to your eyes.* Humble yourself and make every effort to have the contract annulled.

6:6-11 This unit does not fit easily into any of the main forms of wisdom. It is not truly a fable since it does not attribute human characteristics to animals. The ant illustrates a point of unity between all living things and is a rebuke to the lazy person who shows less wisdom than this tiny insect.

6:6 *ant.* The ant is a model of prudent activity (see 30:25). *sluggard.* A lazy person whose relationship to the environment is expressive of life-threatening folly (see 10:26; 13:4; 15:19; 19:24; 20:4; 26:16).

6:7-8 There is irony in the tiny ant showing greater foresight in working in harmony with nature so as to secure its life.

6:10-11 Verse 6 is conceivably an aphorism on its own, and verses 7 to 9 act to give the concrete interpretation. Verses 10 to 11 seem to be an addition by way of application. In 24:33-34 the same saying is applied to a different object lesson.

6:11 *poverty.* Proverbs has much to say about poverty; such a theme illustrates the way proverbial statements have an openness to specific applications. Proverbs warns against the folly that leads to poverty; conversely, diligence and hard work are usually associated with prosperity (see 12:11; 13:4; 14:23). Yet not all poverty is the result of laziness (14:31; 17:5; 19:1, 17, 22; 21:12; 28:3, 11).

6:12-15 Again the form suggests a proverbial saying that has been expanded by the addition of a specific application.

6:12 *scoundrel.* Literally "man of Belial," which is a phrase of uncertain meaning. It probably indicates a worthless person or one who is actively evil. *a corrupt mouth*. Perverse speech that comes from an evil character.

6:13-14 *winks . . . signals . . . motions*. This person will not speak plainly and openly, but makes insinuations and signs that sow the seeds of distrust and dissension.

6:15 *disaster*. The perspective of Proverbs is that of natural retribution built into creation; there is misfortune that is directly related to our foolishness. The Old Testament recognises that ultimately God will punish the wicked (see 24:19-20) and reward the righteous (see 23:17-18; 24:15-16), but it has no real idea of judgment in the afterlife. Therefore, the prosperity of the wicked and the suffering of the righteous posed a serious problem for the Old Testament people of God.

6:16-19 This is the first of the numerical sayings in Proverbs (others are found in 30:15-31). The form may be meant as a kind of riddle in which the answer is given, not to render the riddle a useless exercise but to invite further appropriate answers. It is more likely that it is a method of gathering things that are linked by some common feature. The presupposed orderliness of the universe meant that the making of lists was a fruitful way of underlining previously unrecognised relationships.

6:16 *the Lord hates*. The perspective of this numerical saying contrasts with that of natural retribution in the previous unit (vv. 12-15). Here it is implied that the Lord will judge.

6:20-35 Another warning against adultery that, along with 5:1-23 and 7:1-27, reinforces the seriousness of the matter. The form of this section is a variation of the instruction, using elaborate word pictures to heighten the urgency of the motive clauses (vv. 23, 26, 27-28, 30-31). Although verses 21 to 22 and 23 depend respectively on Deuteronomy 6:8 and Psalm 119:105 which refer to the law, wisdom not law is in mind here. Law is the direct revelation of God; wisdom works within the framework of that revelation to explore the bounds of human responsibility. The law prescribed a judicial punishment for adulterers; wisdom is not soft on adultery but sees the result as the inevitable disaster produced by folly.

6:25 *Do not lust.* Sinful desire is the beginning of folly. The relationship of desire to the act is put most starkly in Matthew 5:28.

6:26 *a loaf of bread.* The Hebrew is not clear; the meaning is probably that of self-induced poverty.

6:27-29 *fire . . . hot coals.* These metaphors are quite clear and emphasise the utter folly of adultery.

6:29 *unpunished.* While Proverbs emphasises natural retribution, from time to time it reminds us that God is judge.

6:30-31 *if he steals to satisfy his hunger.* Stealing when in need is understandable, but it is still subject to the law.

6:32-33 *But a man who commits adultery.* Adultery has no such understandable motive and brings destruction. *blows and disgrace.* See verses 34 and 35.

6:34-35 *fury . . . no mercy.* The jealousy of the offended husband causes a fury that will not be calmed by any offer of compensation. Wisdom frequently examines such dynamics of human behaviour.

7:1-27 There are possibly three originally independent parts to this chapter: verses 1 to 5, 6 to 23, and 24 to 27. Here they are linked by the theme of adultery. The first and third sections are instructions warning against involvement with immorality. The middle dramatic narrative reinforces the instructions.

7:1 *my commands.* See 3:1 and note. *live.* See note on 3:2. *apple of your eye.* Literally "the little man of your eye," a metaphor for the pupil; as the source of sight it must be protected.

7:3 *write them . . . on your heart.* See 3:3 and note. The authority of experience and wisdom points to a life enhancing mode of behaviour.

7:4-5 *sister . . . kinsman.* Pursue wisdom as a way of life rather than be ensnared by the folly of adultery.

7:6-23 The observer in these verses is probably the wisdom teacher.

7:7 *a youth.* Naive and lacking in life's experiences.

7:10-12 *crafty in her intent . . . her feet never stay at home.* The seducer is deceitful, while in reality she is without social roots.

7:13 *kissed him.* She takes a bold approach without giving away her intentions by her facial expression.

7:14 *fellowship offerings.* She appears to be stating a religious intention but her approach suggests that the opportunity for a feast is the real attraction.

7:15 *I came out to meet you.* The young man is flattered with the suggestion that he has been specially chosen.

7:16-17 *my bed.* Then he is offered a sensuous and luxurious experience: the bed will be perfumed with spices.

7:18 *let's drink deep of love.* Here is the real deceit in immorality; the notion that physically oriented romance can satisfy one's deepest longings for mutual love and commitment appeals to the simple. In reality it is a fraudulent claim.

7:19-20 *My husband is not at home.* The seductress tries to allay the young man's fears that the jealous husband may interfere (see 6:33-35).

7:21 *persuasive words.* The power of words for good or evil is a common wisdom theme (see 2:16; 5:3; 10:11; 16:27; 18:21).

7:22 *like an ox going to the slaughter.* The dumb animal is unaware of its fate and allows itself to be led. *like a deer stepping into a noose.* See the NIV text note; the exact meaning is uncertain but refers to walking into a trap.

7:23 *pierces his liver.* A vital organ; the wound is fatal.

7:24 *listen to me.* In contrast to the life-destroying words of the seducer, the words of the wise teacher will lead to life (see 3:1-2).

7:25 *heart.* The centre of the will and understanding. See 2:2 and note.

7:26-27 Wisdom's prescription is to keep one's thought from adultery and to avoid places where there is temptation. *grave. . . death.* See notes on 1:12; 2:18; 5:5.

8:1-21 The typical pattern of the wisdom instruction form is the recommendation of wisdom by the teacher. The basis of wisdom is intellectual reflection on human experience within the framework of the fear of the Lord. Here wisdom is personified as the wisdom teacher and so she recommends herself. In the first section (vv. 1-11) there is a consideration of the human task of learning wisdom. Then (vv. 12-21) there is a statement of the indispensable place of wisdom in the affairs of the world.

8:2-3 See note on 1:21.

8:4 *men.* The Hebrew word usually applies to males, but it may extend to all humanity. Wisdom here does not address sons or pupils but all people. Wisdom should be the property of all human beings, male and female.

8:5 *simple . . . foolish.* See notes on 1:4; 1:22.

8:6-7 *what is right . . . what is true.* "Truth" expresses what is utterly reliable. Proverbs relates truth to wisdom in several places. There is even the suggestion of divine origin in this context.

8:8 *just.* The Hebrew word means "righteousness," which is the opposite of crooked and perverse. In the wisdom context, it refers to the perfect world order created by God and partially preserved despite the corruption of sin.

8:10-11 *silver . . . gold . . . rubies.* Wisdom is often compared to things of great material value (cf. 2:4; 3:14-15; 8:19-21; Job

28:17-19). Here there is also a warning against the false values of materialism.

8:12 See 1:4 and note.

8:13 *To fear the Lord.* See 1:7; 2:5; 9:10 and notes. Wisdom always recognises that the ethical dimension of life has its ultimate foundation in the will and character of the Lord. Although it recognises an authority in experience, it is not an ultimate authority and must always bow to the revealed truth of God. Ethical systems without an absolute standard of right, goodness and truth cannot survive.

8:14 *Counsel.* Wisdom instruction and advice. The counsel of God is his plan and purpose to which true wisdom has access. The perspective on wisdom here sees its close connection with the ultimate reality revealed in the truth of God.

8:15-16 *kings.* The proper function of human rulers is defined by the order of God's creation and the word of God (see Gen 1:26-28). Rulers could depart from wisdom (see e.g. Dt 17:16-17; 1 Sam 8:10-18; 1 Ki 11:1-8; 15:33-34), but wise rule begins with the fear of the Lord (Deut 17:18-20; 1 Ki 3:6-9; 4:29-34). Israel's King-Messiah would rule by perfect wisdom (Is 11:1-3).

8:17 *I love.* While wisdom is hidden from fools (see 1:28-29) she cares for her own (4:6, 8-9). Jesus applied this saying to himself in Matthew 7:7 and thus claimed to be wisdom itself.

8:18-19 *prosperity.* As can be seen from Solomon's early reign, material and social benefits are in keeping with wisdom (see 1 Ki 10). *prosperity.* Hebrew: "righteousness;" a word whose meaning goes well beyond the purely ethical, to include proper order. It includes obedience to God's law, but also extends to right relationships between God, people and creation.

8:20 *righteousness*. The meaning as in verse 18. *justice*. A synonym for righteousness.

8:21 *wealth*. Not the result of shrewd and unproductive speculation which characterises so much wealth in modern western society. It is linked with the ethical values of a wise and God-honouring life.

Selected unit - Proverbs 8:22-31

Description

Although this section has been selected for detailed treatment, it must be seen in the context of the whole of chapter 8. The chapter easily divides into three sections: verses 1 to 21, 22 to 31, and 32 to 36. Even if these were originally three distinct works, they have been brought together here in a way that suggests deliberate purpose.

This section (vv. 22-31) provides the background to the authority of wisdom who calls to be heard (vv. 1-21). The unusual nature of the portrayal of wisdom has provoked much discussion about its intention. If we must chose between poetic metaphor of the wisdom of God and the description of wisdom as a divine attribute with real personality, then the evidence favours the former. Wisdom is depicted as the first of God's creation (vv. 22-23). She then witnessed the creation of all things in the wonderful universe and worked with God in that creation (vv. 24-31). The poem begins and ends with descriptions of wisdom: created before all else, God's craftsman rejoicing in the creation. The centre section (vv. 24-29) emphasises the priority of wisdom over the rest of creation: she was there before anything else existed, and she was there when all things were being made.

The main point of this section is that God is the source of wisdom, and creation is the expression of God's wisdom. The world order established by God at the beginning is the manifestation of his wisdom. The question of folly and its dislocating effects in the world is not raised, for, as Proverbs constantly testifies, God has not allowed such disorder to obliterate the orderliness that makes life possible. Like Psalm 8 or Psalm 19, this poem portrays the work of God in creation as the basis upon which we understand all relationships. The climax in verse 31 points to the dignity of humanity as the pinnacle of creation.

Text

8:22 *The Lord.* Hebrew: *Yahweh*, the personal name of the God of the covenant with Israel (see note on 1:7). This was the name revealed to Moses (see Ex 6:2-5) in the context of God's commitment to fulfil his covenant promises by redeeming Israel out of Egypt. When we take the broad view we see that this is but the continuation of God's original commitment to his creation. *brought me forth*. See the NIV text note. Wisdom is not a divine person but the aspect of God's nature that is expressed in creation and later in redemption. *the first of his works*. The question of how God can create his own qualities is not the point: remember that this is poetic imagery. The poem is emphasising the fact that the whole created universe is based on the wisdom of God that preceded it. This is a commendation of wisdom as our link with reality. *before his deeds of old*. Wisdom comes before everything else God has said or done in his covenant and saving acts.

8:23 *before the world began.* Wisdom is also before the creation of the universe.

8:24 *I was given birth.* The plan of God comes before his action. Reference to birth suggests that wisdom is uniquely the child of God, although this is still a poetic device rather than the claim to be divine.

8:27 *I was there.* By being prior to creation and a participant in the act, the creation is the first demonstration of the wisdom of God. The implication is that wisdom provides the pattern of what is made.

8:28 *fountains of the deep.* A reference to ancient Hebrew cosmology (see Gen 7:11; 8:2).

8:30 *I was the craftsman.* Not merely the witness but the agent of creation. This creative aspect of wisdom is seen in the use of the Hebrew word for wisdom (*hokhmah*) to describe the craftsman's skills in Exodus 31:3.

8:31 *rejoicing. . . delighting.* Wisdom reflects the satisfaction expressed in the divine declaration that creation is "very good" (Gen 1:31).

Function

The whole of chapter 8 is a commendation of wisdom. Placed, as it is, after the warnings against the dangers of the seductress and adulteress, this call of Lady Wisdom is a clear contrast. The chapter division obscures the point but we should see wisdom's call as a challenge to the young man to choose the better way. The motivation is reinforced by this section, for there can be no superior credentials than to be the blueprint of creation.

We may also inquire into the theological function of this significant unit. The Old Testament wisdom literature has always provoked special attention because of the lack of reference to the covenant promises and redemptive history that so characterises the rest of the literature. Proverbs not only shares this lack of covenant theology, but it also has a relative lack of references to God. There are notable exceptions, of which this section is one of the most important. The attempt to put the wisdom thought of Israel into a theology of creation, rather than of redemption, has much to commend it provided we do not judge these two perspectives to be incompatible.

Theologically, then, this passage not only expands the "fear of the Lord" theme, but it reminds us of the inseparable connection of redemption to creation. The presupposition of order that so characterises the wisdom of Proverbs is founded on the creation. "The fear of the Lord is the beginning of wisdom" (9:10) because the same wisdom that established all things in their proper and perfect relationships at the beginning now works to restore them to that order through redemption. Thus, Proverbs 8 is important for grasping the nature of wisdom as a whole.

Testimony to Christ

As stated above, this passage does not support the view that it is speaking of a divine person as such. Yet the reality of God's creative wisdom is eventually given personal expression in the New Testament. There the function of Christ in creation fulfils everything that is stated here of wisdom's role. This is characteristic of the whole progressive revelation of the Bible, in which Christ is finally revealed as the fulfiller of the Old Testament.

When we look at the so-called "cosmic" Christ passages of the New Testament, we are reminded of the pre-existence of the second person of the Trinity, who, in the fullness of time, became a man. In John 1:1-3, Christ the revealing Word is also spoken of as the creator. This connection is not incidental. Also, Paul's description of Christ in Colossians 1:15-16 may have Proverbs 8:22-31 in mind. It certainly indicates that Christ is not only the agent of creation but is also its very reason for being. In a sense Paul is saying that God's ultimate purpose in creation was to bring all things to their fullness through the redemption effected in the gospel. This is utterly consistent with Paul's marvellous exposition elsewhere of the gospel as the wisdom of God and Christ as our wisdom (see 1 Cor 1:21-24, 30). Jesus Christ, being God, perfectly exemplifies the creating-redeeming wisdom of God. As the perfect human being, he is also our wisdom by relating perfectly to God and to the created order on our behalf.

Questions

1. What does this passage teach about the nature of God's wisdom?

2. What function is attributed to wisdom and what does this mean?

3. What is the teaching about creation in verses 30 and 31?

4. How does this passage help us to construct an authentically Christian view of reality?

Comments on Proverbs 8:32-9:18

8:32-35 *Blessed.* See note on 3:13. Blessing is also a covenant idea (see Gen 12:1-3) and contrasts with the curse or judgment that comes upon those who break the covenant (see Dt 28:1-6, 15-19). Here it is probably less a covenant idea than a reference to the benefits of seeking wisdom.

8:34 *watching daily at my doors.* The pupil attends the house of the wise teacher each day.

8:35 *life.* Life means first of all being rightly related to God and, as a result, being rightly related to all people and all things. Without wisdom we exist rather than live, and the apparent order of such existence is soon undone. See also notes on 3:2, 18.

8:36 *fails.* The Hebrew word is that from which "sin" is derived and indicates here a missing of the mark or desired goal. *hate.* To hate wisdom is to hate life itself.

9:1-18 Chapter 9 should probably be read as a whole although it is composite. The effect of it as it stands is to contrast the competing invitations of wisdom and folly, both of whom are portrayed as women calling people to enter their houses. Wisdom invites the simple to eat of her life-giving food (vv. 1-6), while folly conceals the fact that her seemingly desirable food brings death (vv. 13-18). The intervening section (vv. 7-12) may have been added to change the metaphor of wisdom's food in verse 5 into specific examples of wisdom in action.

9:1 *seven pillars.* The meaning is obscure. It may simply indicate the architectural splendour of the house, or it may carry some symbolism which is lost to us.

9:4 *simple.* See 1:4 and note. Compare this with folly's call in verse 16. *lack judgment.* Literally "he who lacks heart," which means not having the will to think and act correctly.

9:5 Compare Isaiah 55:1-2.

9:6 *Leave your simple ways.* See 1:4, 22. *and you will live.* See 2:19; 3:2, 18; 8:35 and notes.

9:7-12 These sayings contrast the wise and the fool.

9:7 *corrects a mocker.* The admonition has no effect; there are some situations where reproof only makes things worse.

9:8 *rebuke a wise man.* By contrast with the mocker, the wise man accepts correction.

9:9 *he will be wise still.* Wisdom observes the principle of human nature that shows us to be either enslaved or liberated. There is no standing still; we progress or regress according to our choice. Wisdom accumulates wisdom (see Mt 13:10-15).

9:10 *The fear of the Lord.* See 1:7 and note. Wisdom and knowledge are the same thing. *Holy One.* Literally "holy ones." The singular reading is based on the parallelism with "the Lord" in the previous line.

9:11 See 3:2 and note.

9:12 *your wisdom will reward you.* See 3:13-18; 4:9-11; 8:35.

9:13-18 This description of folly is in direct contrast to that of wisdom in verses 1 to 6.

9:13 *loud.* Boisterous. *undisciplined and without knowledge.* The sensuous appeal of folly contrasts with wisdom as the teacher of righteousness and order.

9:14 *at the highest point of the city.* Folly is a counterfeit evangelist giving the appearance of being wise (see v. 3).

9:15-16 *Let all who are simple come in here.* A further aping of wisdom (see v. 4).

9:17 *Stolen water.* Anything which is forbidden, especially illicit sex. *food eaten in secret.* Because it is stolen or forbidden. There is a perversity in human nature that is stirred up by prohibition and the law (see Rom 7:7-11).

9:18 *the dead.* Literally "shades," the shadowy existence of the dead. There is no clear teaching in the Old Testament about life after death. Since the blessings and the judgments are expressed in this earthly life, there is no understanding of rewards and punishments in heaven and hell. *the grave.* Hebrew: *sheol*, the place of the departed, whether good or bad. See 1:12; 2:18; 5:5; 7:27 and notes. The significance of Sheol as the destination of fools is not that it is a place of torment, but that those who go there do so prematurely and without knowing the blessings of life through wisdom.

6

One-sentence sayings Proverbs 10:1-22:16

Proverbial wisdom

In chapter 4 above we looked briefly at some of the characteristics of the proverbial or one-sentence sayings that make up a large part of the book of Proverbs. We described the uses of parallelism in such sayings to link things in various relationships and to highlight the contrasts between wise, life-affirming behaviour and foolish, life-destroying behaviour. We also considered how, in the wisdom of Israel, such observations related to the revealed will of God in the law of Moses. (If you have not read that section it would indeed be wise to do so before proceeding with the contents of this chapter.)

The problem before us now is how best to consider the mass of single and unconnected sentences that are contained in this next part of Proverbs. If we treat each saying separately we will no doubt learn something from each; but we also need to ask if this is really the function of such literature. Clearly each saying had its origins quite apart from the others, and that fact alone invites us to consider them in turn. Does this mean, then, that our task is to memorise a multitude of verses against the time when one or other of them might be applicable to some personal experience? There would have been nothing foreign to the ancient Israelite in the idea of learning sayings off by heart.

But even if memorisation is an aspect of the way wisdom was learned, there seems to be something in the nature of the literature that points to another way. Why has the editor of Proverbs gathered his collection the way he has? There is evidence that the editor has made an effort to gather sayings with similar subject matter, yet the effort is not sustained. It also appears that from time to time he has tried to collect sayings with a similar structure without regard to the subject matter. Our consideration of the prologue suggested that there is a teaching purpose in the structure of the book and, if this is so, we must also look for the cumulative effect of the collection.

So, we could set out to comment on these sentence sayings in a number of different ways, each of which would contribute to our understanding. As we would expect, the more technical commentaries follow the book verse by verse, trying to uncover the significance of each verse before attempting some synthesis. This is the approach taken by David Hubbard, dealing with the book thematically section by section. William McKane makes verse by verse comments, but organises the proverbial sentences according to his classification of three main types of wisdom: old wisdom, community concern and Yahwistic piety. Derek Kidner also follows this method but gives an overview of some significant themes as well and a biblical index of themes and ideas. Robert Alden gives a verse-by-verse commentary but also attempts to sum up the key ideas of each unit. Eldon Woodcock provides a topical study that gives a systematic survey of the main ideas in the wisdom of Proverbs. William Mouser arranges his comments not according to subject matter but according to the literary form of the sayings.

(Details of these commentaries are listed at the end of this book.)

In this commentary I am concerned to provide a useful, non-technical tool for understanding not only the content of Proverbs but also how the book may function as Christian Scripture in our lives. While there is much in Proverbs that has a contemporary ring about it, there is also much which reflects the culture and social conditions of ancient Israel. Therefore, understanding what Proverbs can teach us about how we gain and apply wisdom is as important as understanding the specific applications of wisdom in ancient Israel.

We will continue, then, by looking at the contents of Proverbs 10 as one of our selected passages. In so doing we need to remember that chapter divisions were not part of the original and therefore they may give a false impression of the actual structure of the book as a whole. We will also look out for any evidence that the editor of Proverbs has collected this group of sayings on the basis of their content or form.

Selected unit - Proverbs 10:1-32

Description

Strictly speaking, this chapter is not a literary unit. It is a collection of literary units and we want to try to discern if the editor has put them together into any kind of larger unit that functions in a way that the separate parts do not. When we look at the form of these wisdom sentences the most obvious feature is that the majority display *antithetic parallelism*. This shows itself in English translations by a contrast or antithesis in the second part of the verse, being introduced by "but." Thus in the following example the contrast is obvious:

A wise son brings joy to his father,
but a foolish son grief to his mother. (10:1)

The slight variation in the terms of the second part (mother instead of father) is characteristic. Often the contrast is put in terms that have a clear but indirectly stated connection:

Wisdom is found on the lips of the discerning,
but a rod is for the back of him who lacks judgment. (10:13)

This antithetical parallelism continues into chapter 11 and is the predominant form of Proverbs through to the end of chapter 15. There does, therefore, seem to be an editorial purpose in bringing together so many wisdom sentences of the same kind.

This is where one of the differences between wisdom and law emerges. In law, even in areas where natural law might prevail (such as the sanctions against taking life that are to be found in cultures that do not have the revelation of God's law), nothing is left to chance: it is made clear what the will of God is. The application of a specific law may not always be clear in certain circumstances and may require a certain wisdom to perceive the principles at work, but the principles are based on the revelation of God. In wisdom, the principles of God's revelation are one stage removed and provide the general framework within which people work out relationships that affect their lives. In law, the emphasis is on the content, the "what" of God's will for his people. In wisdom, each saying has its "what" but its application is not universal and it can never be taken as a general rule without qualification. The difference is that a law expresses clearly the mind of God while a wisdom saying expresses one human experience in a concrete situation. The proverbial status of these sayings in the collection of wisdom shows that they have become separated from the original life-situation and are open to a wider application. The gathering of wisdom sayings is thus as much concerned with the "how" of gaining wisdom as with the "what" of individual sayings.

Apart from the form of these sayings in our selection, the other obvious aspect to consider is their content. Almost all the antitheses in chapter 10 involve synonyms for "wise" and "foolish," mostly as a contrast of righteous and wicked. Thus it appears that the vocabulary of the sayings may have influenced their selection and inclusion in this chapter.

Text

10:1 *The proverbs of Solomon.* See the discussion of Solomon's authorship in chapter 4 above; see also 1:1 and note. *A wise son.* The definition of wise is here assumed; it is really what the Book of Proverbs sets out to establish. Much about wisdom is learned by examples of wise behaviour and its opposite. Family and personal relationships are important in the expression of wisdom and its effects (see e.g. vv. 5, 8, 13, 14, 19, 21, 23). Here the impact of wisdom, or the lack of it, on one's parents is asserted. Behind this is the recognition of the importance of family relationships and of the need to cultivate them wisely.

10:2 *righteousness.* The most common contrast in this chapter is between the righteous and the wicked. Righteousness in the Old Testament is mainly defined by faithfulness to the law of God. Within wisdom thinking, there is also the general recognition of the order of God's created universe. Righteous thus becomes a synonym for wise, and wicked for foolish. The ethical content of these words is always there, but in wisdom there is often the wider implication of harmony with reality as God has defined it. *delivers from death.* See 2:18; 3:18 and notes.

10:3 *does not let the righteous go hungry.* Proverbs emphasises the natural correlation of wisdom and life. Since it presents no developed idea of life after death within which rewards and punishments occur, the keeping of wisdom is the way to preserve life in the here and now. Behind this natural retribution is the hand of the Lord. Problems therefore arise when the wicked are seen to prosper and the righteous to suffer. This saying, unlike the Book of Job, is not concerned with any exception to the general correlation.

10:4 *Lazy hands . . . diligent hands.* See 6:6-11; 13:4; 15:19; 24:30-34. Poverty is a matter for wisdom's reflection. Poverty itself is no disgrace unless it is due to laziness.

10:5 *a wise son.* Family relationships and their obligations are the key point of this verse rather than the agricultural setting.

10:6 *Blessings.* In wisdom thinking this may refer to the direct blessings of God or the natural outcome of wise living. *violence . . . wicked.* The antithesis with the first line is rather oblique, but see verse 11 where the same phrase is used more appropriately.

10:7 *memory.* How a person is remembered when he is gone. *name.* A synonym for memory, meaning reputation. In Hebrew thought reputation was what survived a person's death. See notes on 1:12; 2:18; 5:5.

10:8 *commands.* Not the law, but the instruction of the wise man (see 3:1 and note). To be teachable is to be wise. *chattering fool.* A person who is too busy talking nonsense to be quiet and listen thus shows he lacks the self-discipline necessary to avoid destruction.

10:9 *The man of integrity walks securely.* Sincerity in life is necessary if one is to avoid pitfalls. The antithesis is the one who perverts the truth and avoids the moral way. He will be found out and disciplined, either by society or by God.

10:10 *winks maliciously.* See 6:13 and note. *chattering fool.* See verse 8 and note. This does not fit the first line as a parallel or contrast. The RSV follows the Greek Old Testament (Septuagint): "but he who boldly reproves makes peace." The contrast here is between a deceitful trouble-maker and a straight-talking healer of relationships.

10:11 *the mouth of the righteous is a fountain of life.* The wise man speaks words which promote life.

10:12 *Hatred.* Rejection of the good order in human relationships. In 1 John 3:15 hate is described as murder. It desires the elimination of all relationships, thus fragmenting society. *love covers.* Wanting the best for others is the greatest expression of ordered relationships. It will overlook matters which cause friction so as to promote harmony in relationships (see Jas 5:20; 1 Pet 4:8).

10:13 The antithetic parallel here is not exact. *Wisdom . . . on the lips.* The perceptive man's character is revealed in the wisdom of his words. *a rod is for . . . him who lacks judgment.* The man who lacks sense simply gets himself into strife. The parallel suggests that his foolish talk is the problem.

10:14 *store up knowledge.* The wise man, though no longer the pupil, will continue to learn. Only a fool thinks he has it all. *the mouth of a fool.* The fool is frequently shown as a babbler (see vv. 6, 8, 13, 18, 19, 31, 32). Knowing when to speak and when to keep silent is a prominent theme in wisdom (see 15:23; 25:11; 26:4-5; Job 38:2; 42:1-6; Ecc 3:7). James, the

"Proverbs" of the New Testament, also explores this theme (see Jas 1:26; 3:1-12).

10:15 *fortified city*. The rich have security against life's uncertainties which the poor are denied. This saying does not moralise on the circumstances of wealth or poverty; this is a simple observation of facts which implies neither the inherent evil of wealth not the inherent virtue of poverty.

10:16 *wages*. The outcome or reward of righteousness is life (see notes on 3:2, 18). *punishment*. Literally "sin", the consequence of which is punishment, the antithesis of life.

10:17 The communal effect of wisdom and folly is important. Wisdom is never a purely private matter, because our style of life sets an example for others. Wisdom as education is highlighted because how one accepts discipline affects others.

10:18 The form of this verse differs from the antithetic parallelism of most of the proverbs in this chapter. The subject is lying or slander; the one who engages in them is either malicious or foolish.

10:19 *The tongue*. See notes on verses 13 and 14. Discipline of the tongue is a mark of wisdom and a disciplined mind, while the babbler displays only his sin.

10:20 *choice silver*. Wise words are worth much. *heart*. Here parallel with the tongue. The mind, will and inner character of the wicked person are the source of his futile words (see Mt 15:18-19).

10:21 *many.* See verses 11 and 17. Wisdom has effects for the good of others. Fools who will not receive wisdom cannot even sustain their own lives.

10:22 *wealth.* See verse 2. In the Old Testament context this would be material wealth, a feature of Solomon's wisdom (see 1 Ki 4:22-28; 10:4-10).

10:23 *evil conduct.* Behaviour which disrupts harmony.

10:24 *dreads.* That which the wicked person fears; not the Lord, but the punishment of the Lord. The implicit meaning seems to be that God's righteous judgment is inevitable.

10:25 *storm . . . stand firm.* Jesus' contrast of the wise and foolish builders in Matthew 7:24-27 may well have been drawn from here. Wisdom is to life as folly is to destruction (see v. 2 and note).

10:26 The form of this proverb differs from the antithetic parallelism of most of the others in this chapter. The effect of the comparison ("as . . . so is . . .") is to invite us to consider the relationship between the pair of items and to determine what they have in common. Thus, vinegar is to teeth as smoke is to eyes, and sluggards to their employers. The structure of the sentence shows that the first line illustrates the second. The lazy employee is a distasteful irritant to his boss.

10:27 *The fear of the Lord.* See 1:7; 9:10 and notes. Harmony with God, here recognised as coming through the provisions of the covenant, means harmony with life. As with the fifth commandment (Ex 20:12) the blessings of God are seen in terms of the promise of the possession of the land. Life after death has yet to be revealed as the sphere of ultimate rewards (see 3:2, 18 and notes).

10:28 Similar idea to verse 27.

10:29 Though also similar to verses 27 and 28, here the basis is the covenant rather than observations of experience. The wisdom literature reminds us from time to time that the source of all true knowledge and wisdom is the revelation of God through his covenant to Israel. See note on 2:20-22.

10:30 See verse 27 and note. Another expression of explicitly covenant-based wisdom. *the land.* Promised to Israel; possession of it is conditional upon the response of faith to the covenant promises.

10:31-32 See verse 14 and note. *perverse.* Speaking crookedly and seeking to prevent sound judgment in others. *cut out.* Either the evil words will be stopped, or the evil speaker will be overthrown.

Function

By being separated from its original concrete experience, the proverbial sentence gives expression to a relationship which occurs in other concrete situations. The form, which is deceptively abstract or general, leaves the saying open to being applied to new life experiences in which the same relationship is perceived to exist. Thus it prompts us to recognise order and the existence of common features in situations that might have appeared on the surface to be different or unrelated. To be able to penetrate to the underlying order by the exercise of wisdom is to be more in command of one's life. Since the underlying order is that established by God, pure self-interest in learning wisdom is ruled out. Righteousness and wisdom are inseparably tied to the character of God, even though in wisdom the link is often assumed rather than expressed.

The collection of these sentences that mostly display the same form (antithetic parallelism) and the same general theme (the contrast of righteousness and wickedness) suggests a particular teaching purpose. The cumulative effect is the cultivation of a way of thinking about life's experiences and about what makes for the good life. The fact that the word "wisdom" in Hebrew covers a broad spectrum of related meanings, from the skill of a craftsman to the keeping of the law of God, reminds us that wisdom is concerned with all dimensions of human life. It is a way of thinking and a way of living; the intellectual and the ethical dimensions must both be recognised.

The nature of antithetic parallelism suggests another aspect of the function of these sayings. Sometimes the contrast is direct and clearly expressed. At other times there is some flexibility in that the contrast is not the direct opposite. For example, there is a direct contrast in:

Lazy hands make a man poor,
but diligent hands bring wealth. (10:4)

But note the oblique nature of the contrast in:

Ill-gotten treasures are of no value,
but righteousness delivers from death. (10:2)

In verse 2 it is not hard to make the link between the ideas in the two halves, yet because there is no direct correspondence of opposites, it remains open to wider application than verse 4.

The oblique contrasts (or *asymmetrical antitheses*) also function to lay bare the real essence of the behaviour in question. In 10:2 the implication of the first line is that unrighteously gained wealth is no real advantage. This seems to contradict human experience which values wealth for wealth's sake, but the antithesis in the second line reminds us of the ultimate values of life and death, and that righteousness is the true life-enhancing wealth.

Another function of a collection such as this is that it shows the broad application of wisdom to life while also highlighting some areas in which it is particularly important for us to cultivate wise thinking and behaviour. Besides the obvious repetition of the wise/fool and righteous/wicked contrasts, we see, for example, various kinds of relationships with other human beings, the importance of diligence in work, and the danger of undisciplined words.

Testimony to Christ

Apart from the obvious cultural and historical gap between ancient Israelite society and our own, it might seem that the proverbial literature needs little or no interpretation in the light of the New Testament. After all, are not almost all of the experiences that are encapsulated in these sayings the common stock of all humanity and largely unchanging through the ages? That is certainly true, and therefore it might seem straightforward that we may apply them to our own situation without trying to find some specifically Christian version of them. To a point that is an acceptable approach, but we must be guided by the New Testament in the matter. How do the proverbial sayings of Israel fit with our life-situation as those who are redeemed by Christ? In previous sections we have looked at some connections between Israel's wisdom and Christ. If, as Jesus taught, all the Old Testament Scriptures testify to him, then the question of how Proverbs is a witness to Christ is very relevant to their use in our lives.

There is little explicit theological teaching in Proverbs 10. I will not go over old ground concerning the relation of empirical wisdom (based on human experience) to the divine wisdom of God's revelation. Let us simply remember that wisdom is portrayed essentially as the gift of God's wisdom in his self-revelation, and the response to this is the human quest for wisdom. It is God's will that redeemed humans express their restored humanity by learning to think and act wisely. This is an important aspect of our sanctification. When we recognise this fact, we see how Old Testament wisdom is one expression of the Bible's teaching about the conforming of the character of God's people to the character of God. The New Testament picks up this theme by showing that the constant failure of Israel to live according to God's revealed will did not thwart God's purposes: Jesus stands in for Israel as the true covenant keeper. He is, as I have mentioned before, not only the wisdom of God come in the flesh, but also the perfecting of human wisdom in response to God's wisdom.

We learn wisdom by meditating on and by applying both the method and the content of Proverbs. This is an aspect of our being restored in our humanity through the salvation we have in Christ. Wisdom is, in other words, part of the process of our sanctification. When properly related to the gospel, it contributes to the renewal of our minds.

Now – and this is crucial – sanctification is our growth in conformity to the image of Christ. Such growth is the fruit of our justification or acceptance by God on the grounds of Christ's merits. So, in this matter, our model for wisdom is Jesus. Proverbs helps us to live wisely in specific responses to specific situations, but we must always have an eye to the greater clarity of the model of wisdom in Jesus. The gospel reinterprets the basic terms of wisdom such as righteousness and wickedness, life and death.

There is also the question of our failure to be wise. As we strive to live wisely, we know we are never totally successful. Wisdom secures life; if, then, we are not immune to the occasional but obvious fit of folly, and since we remain fools to the extent that we remain sinful, how secure is our life before God? The answer is the same for the question of the Christian's failure to be completely free from sin during the process of sanctification: Jesus has fulfilled in our place the perfection God demands. He was the truly wise and fully sanctified human on our behalf. Thus, as we struggle to become wise, we know that our failures do not disqualify us from life because Christ himself is our only qualification. He, when all is said and done, is our wisdom, and to possess Christ is to be accounted wise by the only Judge who matters.

Questions

1. List some of the repeated themes that are found in this section.

2. What are the main contrasts that are dealt with?

3. What things characterise the wise and good life?

4. What is taught here about the use of the tongue?

Comments on Proverbs 11:1-15:33

11:1 *The Lord.* An indication that the covenant is in mind. It was central to the law that Israel's relationship to God in the covenant had implications for relationships among people. Honesty and fair dealing reflect the relationship of God to his people.

11:2 *pride . . . humility.* Self-control is an important theme in wisdom (see 12:16; 29:11). Pride cannot be hidden because it demands expression which others easily read. Note the oblique parallel between disgrace and wisdom (where we might expect honour). In 15:33 honour and humility are linked. Humility means the correct appraisal of one's place in relationship to others, and this promotes a greater sense of the true order of things.

11:3 *integrity.* The Hebrew root means "complete," therefore ethical perfection is in view here. Guidance in living is put in its ethical framework and probably a covenant one at that. A right relationship to the Lord leads to a right course in life.

11:4 *the day of wrath.* A covenantal saying which goes beyond natural retribution to the idea of a personal judge. Wealth cannot secure us against such wrath (see Lk 12:13-21).

11:5 Almost identical with verse 3 (see note).

11:6 Also similar to verse 3.

11:7 *his hope perishes.* Hope is confidence for a future destiny. In Old Testament terms, hope was for a prosperous future as God's blessed people in the promised land. To die young without children and without such fulfilment of God's promises was a tragedy. The prophets projected this hope into a new age, while the New Testament reveals it to be eternal life through resurrection. This verse is a natural sequel to verses 3 to 6 which indicate the life-threatening nature of wickedness.

11:8 *rescued.* The orderly consequences of wisdom, or the providential intervention of God. Such a general consequence is not without contradiction in experience as, for example, when the righteous are perceived to suffer even to death. The Book of Job addresses such a situation, and shows that only trust in the ultimate vindication of the righteous at the hands of a righteous God suffices.

11:9 *With his mouth.* See 10:14, 18, 19 and notes. *knowledge.* Wisdom and knowledge as the way to life enable a person to escape the ways of the godless (see vv. 4, 6, 8).

11:10 *the city.* A viable society must have some recognition of right and wrong and of retribution. It must also approve of retribution as the only just basis for punishment.

11:11 The broader effects of verse 9.

11:12 *tongue.* See verse 9 and note. Gossip and derision will harm others but do not benefit the gossiper. This proverb is one of many dealing with the advantages of knowing when to keep silent (see v. 13; 12:23; 13:3; 17:28; 18:2, 6, 7, 8; Ecc 3:7).

11:13 A variation on verse 12. Maintaining confidences strengthens relationships, but a fool's gossip destroys them.

11:14 *guidance.* A wisdom word meaning wise counsel. See 15:22; 20:18; 24:6. *advisers.* Counsel and advice are features of the emergence of wisdom in political life during the reign of David (see 2 Sam 15:30-17:23).

11:15 See 6:1 and note.

11:16 *kind-hearted.* In their lust for possessions, fools scorn that which is of far greater value: relationships built on respect.

11:17 *benefits himself.* There is legitimate self-interest expressed in the command to "love your neighbour as yourself" (Lev 19:18). What is best for others is best for us.

11:18 *a sure reward.* See 10:2, 16; 2 Cor 9:6-11. The rewards of righteousness have lasting value.

11:19 *life . . . death.* The two ways of living, worked out in specific details in many sayings in this chapter, are here simply stated in the broadest terms. If the covenant framework is present, the principle is the same as that in Deuteronomy 30:15-20. However, righteousness and evil may here be used in the more general wisdom sense and point to the God-given order in existence which experience discerns.

11:20 *The Lord detests.* A covenant-based dogma that proceeds not from human experience but directly from God's revelation. See 3:32.

11:21 *not go unpunished . . . will go free.* The legal terminology suggests that it is the judgment of God that is referred to. It could, however, be a statement on justice in society.

11:22 The form of this saying is the same as several in chapter 25. Two things are placed side by side, inviting comparison. The form is not quite the same as 10:26 which has "as . . . so" to show which is being illustrated by which. Here the two phrases are simply placed together, and it must be questioned whether the translators' provision of "like . . . is" (not in the Hebrew) is helpful or rather forces the interpretation in one direction. The lesson is the incongruity of each situation.

11:23 See 10:24, 25, 28, 29, 30. The contrast of righteous and wicked is seen in the destiny of each.

11:24 This saying is observed to be true at various levels of existence. It applies to sowing and reaping, the use of resources, the use of natural talents, and generosity towards others.

11:25 See verses 17 and 24. The parallelism reinforces the notion that helping others brings benefits to the giver.

11:26 The generous man of verse 25 is illustrated by the community-minded merchant who puts the needs of others above undue profiteering from a manipulated market supply.

11:27 *goodwill.* See verse 17 and note. The reference is either to the benefactor of society who receives community approval in return and his evil opposite, or to the seeker after righteousness who receives the approval of God.

11:28 *whoever trusts in his riches.* See verse 4 and note. When possessions are seen to secure life, God is excluded, and so are right relations with others. The result is the diminution of life.

11:29 *inherit only wind.* The parallelism of this verse is not obvious unless we understand the first line to mean a reckless use of the family wealth that brings ruin on the household. The fool thus inherits nothing and must be the servant of the one who has managed his finances well.

11:30 *The fruit of the righteous is a tree of life.* A curiously mixed metaphor. The result of righteousness is life. See 3:18 and note; also 13:12 and 15:4. *wins souls.* Literally "takes souls" or "takes lives." Normally this means to take away life, but some commentators avoid this by following the Greek (Septuagint) and the RSV in emending "wise" to read "lawless." Thus the second line would read, "but lawlessness takes away lives." The translation remains uncertain.

11:31 *If . . . how much more.* The form of this saying involving intensification is common in wisdom (see 15:11; 17:7; 19:7, 10; 21:27). *the righteous receive their due.* They do not escape either natural or divine retribution. The Greek Old Testament has "If a righteous man is hardly saved," and this is reflected in the quotation of this verse in 1 Peter 4:18. This translation also fits better with the second line. *on earth.* In the land (see 2:20-22 and note).

12:1 Many proverbial sayings are written in an ambiguous way which translators have tended to resolve by supplying their own words. In this saying the Hebrew reads literally "Loving discipline, loving knowledge; but hating correction, stupid." This placing together of things that belong together without indicating which is subject and which is predicate is more open than the expanded English translation allows.

12:2 *A good man obtains favour from the Lord.* Proverbial sayings referring to the Lord can be assumed to have the covenant perspective in view; thus the person here is one who is faithful to the covenant. *favour.* The kindness of God, especially in his saving acts. Those who live by the grace of God will receive grace (see Dt 6:20-25). *crafty.* A man who devises evil schemes (see 1 Cor 6:9-10; Gal 5:19-21).

12:3 See 10:25 and note.

12:4 *a wife of noble character.* See 31:10-31 which is an extended appraisal of such a woman. The woman who so complements her husband is able to achieve fulfilment. *disgraceful.* One who brings shame. This woman destroys her husband's potential and drags him down.

12:5 *plans . . . advice.* Trust must not be based on the outward appearances of a person; one who gives advice may do so with an evil motive (see 10:19-20 and notes).

12:6 *words . . . speech.* See 1:11. The power of words either to heal or to wound is a prominent wisdom theme.

12:7 See verse 3; 10:25 and note.

12:8 *wisdom.* Practical; the person who shows mastery of life is praised. *warped minds.* The inability to think wisely; muddled rather than evil.

12:9 *Better . . . than.* Here is another common proverbial form (see 15:16, 17, 16:8, 19, 32; 17:1). *a nobody.* One who has no social standing or who is not highly regarded by others. *yet have a servant.* The RSV follows the Greek with "who works for himself." The meaning is either "better humble prosperity than poverty concealed by affectation," or "better to work without esteem than to go hungry while dreaming of affluence."

12:10 *cares for the needs of his animal.* Wisdom considers our relationships with the created order and with animals. This is consistent with a concern for righteousness as the established order of all things. The wicked person is not concerned about such relationships and is incapable of kindness.

12:11 *works his land . . . chases fantasies.* The contrast is between the benefits of hard work and the unproductiveness of fantasies.

12:13 See 1:18; 10:11, 14, 31.

12:14 *the fruit of his lips.* Wise speech creates good relationships; its rewards are as tangible as those of physical labour.

12:15 *listens to advice.* See verse 1. While the fool thinks he knows better, the wise man is humble enough to learn from the experience of others. He also is able to recognise what is good counsel.

12:16 Another important theme of wisdom is personal self-control (see 11:2; 29:11). The fool reacts immediately and in a way that prevents a restoration of relationships; the wise person leaves the door open to reconciliation.

12:17 *truthful . . . honest.* On first sight this proverb is a mere tautology, but it actually expresses the relationship between character and deeds (see v. 5 and note).

12:18-19 These two sayings enlarge on the theme of verse 17. They consider the effects of words on personal relationships (v. 18), and the strength of truth over lies which give themselves away (see v. 13).

12:20 *deceit.* The contrast with joy suggests that self-deceit is intended. *peace.* The Hebrew word *shalom* means "wholeness" and is a relational term rather than one of subjective feeling.

12:21 *No harm befalls the righteous.* The normal expectation of the wise and righteous is that they avoid life-threatening situations. The problem of righteous suffering must be seen within the framework of this norm and not as a denial of it. Job's friends made the unwarranted deduction that this is a rigid rule and that suffering must be an indicator of evil-doing.

12:22 *The Lord detests lying lips.* The motive for truthfulness is above all the revealed character of the God of truth.

12:23 *keeps his knowledge to himself.* This is an expression of discretion rather than selfishness. Wisdom learns when to keep silent and when to speak (see 26:4-5; Ecc 3:7). By contrast, the fool has such an inflated idea of his cleverness that he must show off. He thus shows only his foolishness.

12:24 Hard work leads to mastery of life while slackness gets a person into debt.

12:25 *a kind word.* In James 2:15-16 we are reminded that the ministry of encouragement is far more than speaking a superficial word; yet the spoken word is still an important aspect of caring for one another.

12:26 The Hebrew of the first line is obscure. The NIV text note gives a possible translation which fits the antithetic parallelism of the second line.

12:27 *roast.* The Hebrew is uncertain but possibly reads, "The lazy man will not succeed in snaring his supper."

12:28 *life.* See 3:2, 18 and notes. *immortality.* Literally "not death." See 2:18 and note; also 3:2. A comparison of the NIV and the RSV shows the difficulty in translating this line. If the

NIV is accepted, we should note that immortality is not the developed New Testament idea of eternal life. In this context it may mean that the wise man avoids untimely death.

13:1 The humility involved in being teachable is a mark of wisdom, while a fool only scoffs at correction (see 1:7, 22).

13:2 *the fruit of his lips.* The power of words is a popular wisdom theme (see 10:11, 13, 19; 12:14 and notes). Wise words are constructive and the speaker himself benefits from their effects. *unfaithful.* Treacherous, deceitful; those whose social conscience is warped.

13:3 *guards his lips.* Exercising self-control in speech so that what is said is carefully weighed for its possible effects. *speaks rashly.* Hasty or malicious words used without concern for the consequences.

13:4 *sluggard.* See 6:6, 9-11; 12:27 and notes. Human responsibility cannot be avoided. Neither the world nor God owe us a living. *diligent.* With no illusions about labour and rewards, the diligent person engages reality and is sustained.

13:5 See 10:2 and note. *brings shame and disgrace.* Literally "causes a stink and brings shame or scandal."

13:6 See 10:9; 11:3-9 and notes.

13:7 *One man . . . another.* A characteristic of proverbial sayings is their openness to different interpretations or applications. Here the specific observation involving two particular people clearly does not present itself as a general rule. No explicit judgment is being made. There is a contrast in the possessions of each, but the point of the proverb seems to be in the similarity of pretence. There is also a loss of perspective and realism that suggests folly.

13:8 *no threat.* A poor person does not have to worry, as a rich person does, about being kidnapped for ransom. The principle here is that the security of riches can be a threat while the insecurity of poverty has at least one advantage.

13:9 *shines brightly.* Literally "rejoices." The metaphor probably refers to the houses of the two kinds of people. The house symbolises life; one prospers and the other is cut short.

13:10 The proud and arrogant show only contempt for wisdom (see 11:2 and note).

13:11 *Dishonest money.* Either gained fraudulently or speculatively. *little by little.* Through honest hard work. Different money-making methods betray either a wise or a foolish attitude to life.

13:12 *Hope deferred.* Human experience teaches us that frustrated expectations may cause a loss of morale and a sense of hopelessness. The proverb is not suggesting instant gratification of all our wants, but rather that it is important to have right and realistic goals in life. *tree of life.* See 3:18 and note.

13:13 *will pay for it . . . is rewarded.* One of the main themes of proverbial wisdom is the link between deeds and their outcome, whether seen as natural retribution or divine justice.

13:14 *fountain of life.* See 10:11 and note. *snares of death.* The fool tends to trap himself (see 1:17-18).

13:15 The parallelism is indirect: the person with the ability to make sound judgments gains approval, while the one who has a warped perspective takes the path to ruin.

13:16 This saying may appear to state the obvious but, as with 12:17, it expresses the relationship between a person's inner character and deeds.

13:17 *A wicked messenger.* The one who brings a deceitful message often finds that the lie rebounds to his own hurt. Such a messenger was the Amalekite who falsely claimed to have killed Saul, thus hoping to win favour from David, but who was executed for his trouble (see 2 Sam 1:1-16). *healing.* The true messenger promotes the welfare of others.

13:18 See 1:20-33 and notes.

13:19 See verse 12 and note. The achievement of a worthwhile goal has benefits for one's life. Fools will not turn from evil to pursue such goals.

13:20 *walks with the wise.* We become like the company we keep.

13:21 See verse 16 and note.

13:22 *an inheritance for his children's children.* Wisdom in life has lasting effects, especially in one's family. On the other hand, the effect of folly is that one's wealth is dissipated. *stored up for the righteous.* The wealth lost to the fool will be acquired by wise people.

13:23 *injustice.* Here a new dimension complicates the pattern of natural retribution: the natural relationship between hard work and sufficiency is thwarted by oppression.

13:24 *rod.* The word is almost certainly used here as a metaphor (cf. Mic 5:1) for any kind of discipline and correction. The relationship of discipline and love prevents such correction from being destructive.

13:25 See verses 13, 18, 21 and notes.

14:1 *The wise woman.* Refers either to the virtuous wife and mother or to wisdom itself (see 9:1). If the latter, the house is the life of the wise.

14:2 *upright.* The wise, ethically honest person. *fears the Lord.* See 1:7 and note.

14:3 *A fool's talk.* See 10:13 and note. Gossip and foolish talk bring trouble to those who indulge in them.

14:4 *empty.* The Hebrew is obscure, perhaps meaning "clean" – no oxen means no mess! But, no oxen also means no ploughing and so no crops. In other words, no investment leads to no profit.

14:5 See 12:5, 17 and notes.

14:6 *seeks wisdom and finds none.* The mocker does not have the humility to learn from wisdom and only seeks it for short-term gain.

14:7 Not a proverb but an instructional command. See notes on 1:8-9.

14:8 *prudent.* One who acts with real shrewdness. Fools deceive themselves.

14:9 The Hebrew of this verse is obscure (cf. RSV). *making amends.* Fools do not want to restore relationships whereas the wise work at them.

14:10 *Each heart knows its own bitterness.* While much wisdom reflects on interpersonal relationships, there is also a concern for those aspects of life that are personal and private. Some things cannot be communicated and we must learn to know what they are.

14:11 See 10:25 and note.

14:12 *a way that seems right.* The implication is that what may seem right is not necessarily so if the judgment is not made according to true wisdom. Such a way cannot promote life.

14:13 *in laughter the heart may ache.* Like verse 10 this is also a reflection on the personal aspects of life. Life is such that there can never be joy which is completely isolated from grief.

14:14 The Hebrew of the second line is obscure. As it stands it is a typical expression of the order that brings its own retribution.

14:15 *believes anything.* Uncritical acceptance of information is compared with the careful testing of what is said before acting on it.

14:16 Although not in the Hebrew text, "the Lord" is inserted by the NIV after "fears," but the parallelism of the second line favours the RSV translation: "A wise man is cautious and turns away from evil."

14:17 *quick-tempered.* One who loses control easily. *crafty.* The Hebrew word is usually translated "discretion" which is a positive virtue (see 1:4; 2:11; 3:21; 5:2; 8:12). The RSV has "man of discretion" and this would be supported by the parallelism in that version. *hated.* The RSV follows the Greek and translates this as "patient." The NIV follows the Hebrew text and implies "hated by fools."

14:18 *The simple.* Here not merely unskilled but probably rash in making decisions.

14:19 *bow down.* Probably a reference to the grudging respect that evil men must have for the good. It could also refer to the justice of God when the good are vindicated and the wicked made to bow before them.

14:20 People eventually tire of friendships that are always making demands. It is easy to maintain relationships when one is self-sufficient.

14:21 This proverb may have been placed next to verse 20 to provide a moral framework for friendships. The covenant established kindness and the care of one's neighbour based on the grace of God. This principle is sharply in focus in the New Testament where the gospel requires that we treat each other in a way that reflects God's treatment of us through Christ (e.g. 1 Jn 4:7-11).

14:22 *plot.* The skill of evil people is misguided. *love and faithfulness.* A phrase used of God's loving compassion for his covenant people, here applied to the highest human love and loyalty.

14:23 See 10:4; 12:11, 27; 13:4 and notes.

14:24 Similar in meaning to verse 23. The second line emphasises the futility of the life-style of a fool.

14:25 See verse 5. The first line expresses the results of truthful witness in a legal dispute. The second line does not complete the antithesis but indicates the nature of false witness as it obscures the truth.

14:26 *a secure fortress.* The wise man by his wisdom provides a secure home for his children and guards them from harm.

14:27 *The fear of the Lord.* Synonymous with wisdom. The source of true life and, therefore, the way to avoid destruction.

14:28 *a king's glory.* The wisdom of Israel often reflects on the rule of kings. The glory of Solomon as king depended on his people as the main resource of national wealth.

14:29 Similar to verses 16 and 17.

14:30 *A heart at peace.* A person's inner harmony of thoughts, will and emotions has beneficial effects on bodily health. The reverse is also true (see 3:7-8).

14:31 See verse 21 and note.

14:32 See 1:26-27 and notes. *death.* The RSV follows the Greek and reads "integrity" which suits the parallelism better. The NIV translates the Hebrew as "death." This does not necessarily indicate an understanding of life after death, but it does express confidence that the righteous are vindicated.

14:33 See the NIV text note. *lets herself be known*. Either the fool brags about his wisdom, or even fools are forced to recognise wisdom.

14:34 *exalts*. Either morally or as the operation of divine retribution (see Dt 28:1-14; 1 Ki 4:20-28). *disgrace*. Disgrace invites retribution (see Lev 20:17).

14:35 *a wise servant*. The wisdom of the royal court demands appropriate behaviour in a servant. This is not merely the avoidance of the king's wrath, as the implication is that the king is concerned for wise rule.

15:1 *A gentle answer . . . a harsh word*. The power of the spoken word is an important wisdom theme (see vv. 2, 4, 14, and 23). Language is basic to human relationships but can be used for good or ill.

15:2 See 6:17, 24; 10:20, 31; 12:18-19. The wise person thinks well and speaks accordingly.

15:3 See 2 Chronicles 16:9; Psalm 33:13-14. Wisdom from time to time reflects on the reality that is greater that human experience. God's justice is real.

15:4 A contrast of the use of words; they can either build people up and enhance their lives, or destroy them (see 12:18-19). *tree of life*. See 3:18 and note.

15:5 See 1:8; 6:20; 12:15; 13:1, 13, 18. A wise person is humble and teachable.

15:6 *treasure*. Either material riches (as in 1 Ki 4:20-28), or metaphorical for wisdom (see 8:18-21).

15:7 See verse 2 and note.

15:8 *sacrifice*. See Isaiah 1:12-13; Amos 5:21-22. The cultic provisions of the law are part of the revealed wisdom of God. The folly of the wicked is to think that formal and outward adherence to the law can benefit them in any way at all. The prayer of the upright, however, expresses in worship what the fear of the Lord is.

15:9 Similar to verse 8 but without the cultic reference (see 12:2 and note).

15:10 *path*. The way of wisdom (see 2:12-15). Discipline will be needed to get back onto the path (see v. 5; 12:1).

15:11 *Death*. Hebrew: *sheol*, the place of the departed (see 1:12). *Destruction*. Death as the destruction of life. The Lord knows the secrets of the grave; how much easier is it for him to know what is in our minds (see Ps 139:23-24).

15:12 *mocker*. See 1:22. Pride and stupidity go together.

15:13 See 14:30 and note. The way we think and our bodily health can often be seen to correlate.

15:14 *the mouth of a fool feeds on folly*. The wise man nourishes his words on true knowledge.

15:15 See verse 13; 14:30 and notes.

15:16 For other examples of "better ... than" comparisons see 12:9; 15:17; 16:8, 19, 32; 17:1, 12, 19:1. *little ... great*. The relationship of wisdom to material wealth varies. Here wisdom accompanies a frugal life-style but is more than adequate compensation.

15:17 *a meal of vegetables.* The quality of personal relationships does not depend on wealth. Hospitality is more than the provision of good food.

15:18 See 14:17, 29; 15:1. *a patient man.* Another important wisdom theme is that of the "cool" person. When passions are controlled and patience exercised, we find we can disagree without being disagreeable.

15:19 See 6:6-11; 10:4; 13:4. *the sluggard.* Here seen as the opposite of the upright. The lazy person makes no effort to establish a way in life; the righteous (diligent) person removes the obstacles to a fulfilling life.

15:20 See 10:1 and note.

15:21 See 10:23 and note.

15:22 See 11:14; 13:10 and notes. *many advisers.* An argument for the implementation of collective wisdom.

15:23 *joy.* There is great satisfaction in being able to give a wise word at the right time.

15:24 See 2:18-22 and notes. *grave.* See 1:12 and note.

15:25 This is not a saying based on observed facts so much as a declaration of the judgment of God (see 14:11). *the widow's boundaries.* See Deuteronomy 19:14; 27:17. Since the oppression of widows was a fact (e.g. Isa 1:17, 23; 10:2), this saying must be seen as expressing confidence in the ultimate justice of God.

15:26 *pleasing to him.* The ultimate wisdom is to find acceptance with God (see vv. 8-9).

15:27 *greedy*. The parallel in the second line suggests a person whose riches are ill-gotten and who takes bribes. Our folly always has its repercussions on those closest to us (see 1:19).

15:28 See verse 2 and note. The circumspect word of wisdom requires careful thought about the consequences before it is uttered.

15:29 See verse 8 and note.

15:30 See verse 13 and note. *A cheerful look*. Literally "the light of the eyes," which is obscure. Perhaps the radiance of the one who bears good news, or a pleasant sight. Thus, either to see a cheerful (radiant) person or a beautiful scene affects one's mind in the same way that good news promotes our general well-being.

15:31 *He who listens to a life-giving rebuke*. It is a mark of wisdom to be able to accept correction.

15:32 *He who ignores discipline*. To ignore discipline is to forgo its benefits for one's life. This is the ultimate in self-neglect.

15:33 *The fear of the Lord*. See 1:7 and note.

Selected unit - Proverbs 16:1-15

Description

The *aphorisms*, or proverbial sentences, continue. In this section the antithetic parallelism that has characterised the collection in chapters 10 to 15 is not so prominent; in fact, only two of the fifteen sayings have that structure (vv. 1-2). In verse 3 it appears that we have a fragment of an instruction containing the imperative and the consequences. Sometimes the parallelism in the second line does not contrast (antithetic) or restate (synonymous) the thought of the first line, but develops it (synthetic):

The Lord works out everything for his own ends -
even the wicked for a day of disaster. (16:4)

Sometimes the synonymous parallelism seems to merge with a kind of synthetic statement by clarifying the first line:

The lips of a king speak as an oracle,
and his mouth should not betray justice. (16:10)

These various kinds of parallelism provide different ways of looking at reality and of relating it to the perceptible order of things. However, this section provides us with a variation more significant than that of the actual forms. The editor has gathered a number of sayings with a very deliberate theological content, and some contemplate the ideals of human leadership.

Some commentators (e.g. William McKane) have tried to show that the sentence literature can be grouped according to purpose and betrays an historical development. Thus there are the secular sentences of old wisdom which aim to equip the individual for the good life, then there is a concern for community life, and finally a reinterpretation of the older empirical wisdom so that it fits with the theological ideas of the covenant.

However, such evolutionary analysis is unconvincing. There is no firm evidence that certain more complex forms of wisdom saying depend upon simpler ones. Both the longer instructions and the short sayings exist in the wisdom literature of Israel's neighbours and predate their use in

Israel. We must also reject the thoroughly discredited notion that there is an evolution of ideas from the secular to the more theological. Such a view ignores the nature of special revelation and reduces it to the level of merely human religious thought. Thus we must allow that individual training for life, community concerns and reflection on the word of God in relation to human existence all belong together in Israelite society from the beginning. The historical question of the development of wisdom thinking and literary forms must be pursued on firmer assumptions.

In this selection verses 1 to 7, 9 and 11 make specific reference to "the Lord." A number of sayings in chapter 15 make similar reference (15:3, 8, 9, 11, 16, 25, 26, 29, 33). We have seen repeatedly how Proverbs is constructed under the overarching idea of the fear of the Lord, showing the concern of the final editor to place all wisdom, even the most secular-sounding empirical sayings, within the framework of the covenant. We need to keep on reminding ourselves of this viewpoint because of the tendency we have today to divide our thinking up into our day-to-day secular thinking and so-called spiritual thinking. Proverbs reminds us that we are not necessarily unspiritual if we don't mention God in every second sentence we utter. What is really unspiritual is to have two separate realities that we operate under, so that we fail ever to recognise the function of the fear of the Lord in the ordinary mundane matters of life.

Text

16:1 See also verses 2 and 9. God created us in his image and made us responsible, reasoning beings. This points to the ongoing tension in experience between the sovereignty of God and the responsibility of mankind. Wisdom is especially mindful of the task we have to think through issues, make decisions and then bear the responsibility for the outcome. This proverb reminds us that we must make well-considered plans while all the time God is in control of all that happens. *from the Lord comes the reply of the tongue.* This means either that God enables us to give the appropriate answer or carry through our plans, or that God's answer from his word is the real power that shapes events (see Phil 2:12-13).

16:2 See 21:2. *motives.* Literally "spirit" (see RSV). There is a limit to human wisdom even in understanding our own motives. God knows the secrets of our hearts in a way we never can.

16:3 This fragmentary instruction implies an understanding of the fear of the Lord. *Commit.* Literally "roll." This is an unusual idiom suggesting the bringing of all we do to God for his prior approval. To commit our deeds to him means that we allow God's word to be the supreme guide and we apply his revelation to our plans. When we do this our efforts are not in vain.

16:4 *his own ends.* Literally "his (or its) answer." The disruption of the created order because of sin does not thwart divine justice; the Lord makes everything with its fitting retribution. This saying seems to anticipate the carefully worked out theology of retribution in Romans 9:21-23.

16:5 See 11:20-21 and notes.

16:6 *Through love and faithfulness.* This is the attitude of the wise towards God and his revealed will. It is synonymous with its parallel, the fear of the Lord (see 3:3; 14:22; 20:28). A purely formal or ritual approach to God has no validity, for love and faithfulness express a personal attitude to the person of God.

16:7 *pleasing to the Lord.* This probably means that a wise life-style that accepts reconciliation and friendship with God will also work for reconciliation with others.

16:8 See 15:16-17 and notes.

16:9 See verses 1 and 2 and notes.

16:10 *The lips of a king.* This proverb reflects the importance of the king as God's anointed in Israel. Royal wisdom was seen in David who spoke as a messenger of God (see 2 Sam 14:17, 20), and in Solomon (see 1 Ki 3:9). Although the king had a unique place in the plan of God for his people, all leaders share the responsibility to seek both the gift of God's wisdom through his word, and the wisdom that is obtained through their own efforts.

16:11 See 11:1; 20:10, 23; Amos 8:5. *Honest scales.* Weights and measures are based on the order which makes life meaningful. God has established this order and maintains righteous standards. To act unjustly in this regard is to encourage chaos. The law against false weights is found in Leviticus 19:35-36 and Deuteronomy 25:13-16.

16:12-13 *Kings.* Wisdom concerning kingship not only reflects the ideal of Solomon and his wise rule, but also expresses the power of the king to establish righteous order in his realm.

16:14 *A king's wrath.* While it is possible that the wrath of the king is here regarded as righteous anger bringing destruction to those who refuse wisdom, it is more likely that the unrighteous wrath of the king is in view. Such passion does not work wisdom and makes for deathly disorder. *a messenger of death.* For those who are subject to absolute rule, the unjust wrath of the ruler is something to be avoided and great wisdom is needed by those who suffer it.

16:15 A reflection of the power of the king in ancient society. He is able to bestow favours and to promote the careers of his servants.

Function

As we noted in the description of this text, there are two main perspectives included in this group of sentences: royal wisdom and theological wisdom. Both are important for enabling us to deal with the matter of how empirical wisdom (that which we learn through our senses and experience) relates to the revelation of God and his wisdom. This has always presented something of a problem, so that many books written on the theology of the Old Testament have expressed difficulty in fitting the wisdom literature into a general theological scheme.

In the context of the Book of Proverbs, these sentences may be seen as reminders of the theological roots of wisdom. The heyday of wisdom occurred in relationship to the flourishing of the office of king, during the reigns of David and Solomon. In the introductory chapters 2 and 3, we saw that kingship was integral to the order that God had ordained for his people and that it is a key office that foreshadows the person and work of Christ. Solomon brought old and empirical wisdom into the context of his rule and of the temple which was the symbolic heart of the revelation of God. When we look at the sentences in 16:1-15 we find these three dimensions: God, the king, and the subjects of both God and king.

The most prominent teaching about the Lord in this section is that he is sovereign; that is, he is in complete control of all things. This means that there are two kinds of limits on human wisdom. The first is that even when we use our minds and reasoning powers to choose a course of action, God is in control of the process right through to the outcome. The second limit, not prominent in Proverbs, is that there are areas of mystery where God alone is in control and all we can do is trust him. The Book of Job addresses this aspect of wisdom.

Thus, one of the riddles of Christian existence is faced and partially answered here. The relationship of God's sovereignty to human responsibility has always been perplexing. The popular but quite unbiblical solution is to arrange a kind of compromise: God forgoes some of his control so as to accommodate our freedom to act responsibly. This view assumes that to maintain the absolute sovereignty of God is to reduce humans to puppet status and therefore to remove all responsibility from us. This is an error that is compounded by the notion that we must be absolutely free if we are to be held responsible for our actions. Proverbs, however, within its own wisdom context, recognises that our lack of freedom is blameworthy because we have brought it upon ourselves. In more deliberately theological terms, we would have to consider this matter in terms of the fall of humanity into sin. This is a moral revolt against God that results in the bondage of our wills.

The other subject addressed in this section is kingship. Israel's king was chosen to represent the rule of God in the midst of his people. During Solomon's reign the kingly rule and the priestly ministrations at the temple were related in a significant way. The narrative account of the wisdom of Solomon in 1 Kings 3 to 10 includes an extensive treatment of the building and dedication of the temple. The glory and function of the temple were perceived as expressions of the wisdom that Solomon received from the Lord (see 1 Ki 5:7, 12). The main principle of wisdom, 'the fear of the Lord,' is defined by the ministry of reconciliation at the temple (see 1

Ki 8:37-43). The temple, along with the rule of Solomon, was part of the outward expression of Solomon's wisdom that was exhibited to the Gentiles (see 1 Ki 10:1-9). The proverbs of royal wisdom, then, function as a way of pointing to the ideals of leadership that are established to preserve the proper order of human society but which may be abused and exercised in unrighteousness. Human government is meant to reflect the just rule of God.

Testimony to Christ

What has been said regarding previous selected sections concerning their testimony to Christ also applies here. However, the specific themes of this selection are important for their Christological significance; that is, for how they prepare the ground for understanding who Christ is. Of course, Christ in his gospel provides us with the full basis of understanding how these texts apply to us as Christian Scripture.

First, as already noted, Jesus Christ is seen as the Lord of the Old Testament, the creator and the giver of the covenant to Israel. The gospel requires us to make the distinctions between the Father, the Son, and the Holy Spirit. Nevertheless, the 'Lord' spoken of in Proverbs (and everywhere else in the Old Testament) is revealed finally as Jesus Christ. So for a Christian to "fear the Lord" is to believe the gospel and to seek to live consistently with it.

Then, we see Jesus as the true Israelite or the perfect human (or the last Adam). This union of true God and true man in the one person, Jesus of Nazareth, helps us to grasp the significance of the insoluble mystery of how God can remain sovereign and still hold us responsible. The gospel does not show us how this can be so; that is something knowable only by God. But it does give us the clearest possible perspective: Jesus is both true (sovereign) God and true (responsible) man. To weaken either the divine sovereignty or the human responsibility is to destroy the gospel. Thus, in Christ we have the pattern of the divine-human relationship as it ought to be. These proverbs that speak, on the one hand, of the responsibility we have to make decisions and to act, and, on the other, of the overriding sovereign rule of God, are thoroughly consistent with the perspective given in the gospel.

Finally, we note that Jesus comes as the only king of Israel to rule perfectly according the ideals of kingship set out in Deuteronomy 17:14-20. He is the true son of David, thus fulfilling that role in a way that sinful Solomon could never do. He is the wise king who shows the ultimate wisdom by his gospel. He is the new temple and builds the church as the dwelling place of God. The key point in all these matters is that the people of God exercise royal wisdom by being united to Christ by faith and by living by the gospel.

The proverbial statements extolling the role of the kingship may be looked at in the larger contemporary context of human government and leadership. But this can be done only when we first consider the ministry role of Jesus as exemplifying the will of God for the human race. The ramifications are too numerous to take up here. However, the purpose of God to bring all things into subjection to Christ points us beyond the question of church government to the proclamation of the Kingdom of God in all the world.

Questions

1. What is the nature of God's sovereign control over all things?

2. What is the relationship between God's sovereignty and human responsibility as shown in this section?

3. How does the king figure here? Does this teaching apply only to Israel's king or to all human leaders, and why?

4. Does the kingship of Christ and his wisdom affect our understanding of these proverbs? If so, how?

Comments on Proverbs 16:16-22:16

16:16 Several proverbs use the "better . . . than" comparison. These clearly state the superiority of one thing over another; the challenge is to understand why this is so. That wisdom is better than material riches is a common theme in Proverbs (e.g. 3:13-15; 8:10-11, 19). This does not mean that riches are themselves undesirable (so 3:9-10; 1 Ki 3:10-13; 10:7-9), but only that they must be acquired as the fruit of wisdom.

16:17 See 15:19 and note.

16:18 See 11:2 and note. Pride makes a person unteachable and is therefore destructive folly.

16:19 See 15:16 and note.

16:20 *instruction.* Probably the instruction of the wise man, but line two makes it clear that such instruction is given in the context of the revealed word of God. Trusting in the Lord is the same as fearing the Lord (see 1:7 and note).

16:21 The wise gain a reputation for astuteness. *pleasant words.* Literally "sweet" or "honeyed;" words which reflect an aptitude for communication. *instruction.* What is taken in. Thus, the persuasiveness of the teacher increases what is learned by the pupil. Such a teacher is an example of the wise man in the first line.

16:22 *fountain of life.* Source of life (see 10:11). *folly brings punishment to fools.* The Hebrew is ambiguous. The more natural meaning is "the disciplining of fools is folly," that is, it is a waste of time because they do not have the humility to receive it.

16:23 *heart.* See note on 2:2. The wise man speaks out of a mind which is properly informed. *instruction.* See note on verse 21. His wise words command acceptance.

16:24 *pleasant words.* See note on verse 21. A reference to the power of the right words to heal relationships and promote well-being.

16:25 See 14:12 and note.

16:26 *The labourer's appetite works for him.* The threat of hunger is the strongest possible motive for hard work (see 2 Thess 3:10-12).

16:27 *scoundrel.* A destructive person (see 6:12 and note). Words also can be used to destroy relationships.

16:28 A more specific expression of the meaning of verse 27.

16:29 *A violent man.* The violence may lie in the result of the deception. The picture is of a person who uses deceit to lead another astray.

16:30 See 6:13 and note.

16:31 *Grey hair*. The normal expectation is that wisdom and righteousness lead to a long life (see 3:2 and note); thus there is honour attached to old age because of experience, learning and wisdom.

16:32 *a patient man*. One who is not easily provoked. He brings calm and sound judgment to a crisis (see Jas 1:19-20). *controls his temper*. Wisdom does not excuse lack of control on the basis of temperament. Self-control is a skill to be learned.

16:33 *The lot*. Uric and Thummin (see Ex 28:30; Num 27:21; 1 Sam 28:6). These were probably small stones that were withdrawn from the priest's robe to indicate God's guidance. The lot, like tossing a coin, could be used simply to avoid human bias and to ensure equal opportunity, but when the lot was properly used the answer was not a matter of chance but from God. This proverb cannot justify such methods now as the very limited use of the lot passed with the gospel. The use of the lot in Acts 1:26 is a special case occurring between the going of Jesus and the coming of the Holy Spirit.

17:1 See 15:16-17; 16:8, 19. *feasting with strife*. Literally "sacrifices of strife." The parallel in the first line shows that a meal is indicated. It is probably intended to contrast with the fellowship meal of the peace offering (see Deut 27:7). Harmony and fellowship are not dependent on elaborate meals.

17:2 See 11:29. Inherited privilege can easily be forfeited to those who by diligence show themselves worthy to enjoy it.

17:3 *The crucible . . . the furnace.* Fire does not destroy precious metals but refines them. In like manner, the Lord uses our testing experiences to improve us. The conjunction at the beginning of line two can be translated "and."

17:4 Compare 12:18; 15:4; 16:27. The sin is not simply in the listening but in the implied perverse desire to use for evil what is heard.

17:5 See 14:21 and note; 14:31.

17:6 *Children's children.* See Psalms 127:3; 128:1-6. The natural desire of all parents to have grandchildren was intensified in Israel where the full blessings of the covenant, which lay in the future, were to be possessed by one's descendants. *parents are the pride.* See Exodus 20:12. Parents are honoured as the guardians and most influential teachers of their children. In Israel the faithful would defer to their parents as those who would pass on to them wisdom and knowledge of the covenant.

17:7 *how much worse.* Or "how much more . . . " is a literary device used in some proverbs to emphasise a comparison (see 11:31; 15:11; 19:7, 10). *Arrogant.* The RSV translates this as "fine." See the NIV text note. Since the point is that certain kinds of speech are out of character with certain kinds of people, the RSV is to be preferred.

17:8 *A bribe is a charm.* Bribery is effective. As in some other proverbs, this is only an observation of what happens without any moral judgment.

17:9 See 10:12 and note.

17:10 The wise man is humble enough to learn from a rebuke whereas a fool will not be changed by more severe measures (see 9:7-9).

17:11 Government is given by God for the preservation of order in society (see Rom 13:1-5). Rebellion invites official retribution against the attempt to destroy social order.

17:12 *A bear robbed of her cubs*. An enraged bear is less danger to life than folly (see 2 Sam 17:8).

17:13 The person who is so alienated from others that he repays evil for good makes it impossible for people to do him good.

17:14 Compare 15:18. *like breaching a dam*. What starts as an apparently insignificant trickle soon leads to a burst of destruction.

17:15 The justice of God is meant to be reflected in social order and justice.

17:16 *money in the hands of a fool*. Merely paying school fees will not get you wisdom.

17:17 *a brother is born for adversity*. A true friend or brother will stick by you even in times of trouble.

17:18 See 6:1-3 and notes.

17:19 English translations tend to obscure the nature of this proverb by indicating the subject ("He who . . . ") and the predicate. The Hebrew simply places the four things side by side: "loving strife, loving sin, making his gate high, seeking destruction." The wisdom application is the discerning of the common element in all of them.

17:20 See verse 13. Social relationships are essential for life; to destroy them is to invite disaster.

17:21 See 10:1 and note; 15:20; 17:25.

17:22 See 14:30; 15:13, 30 and notes.

17:23 See verse 8 and note.

17:24 The contrast is between concentration on the task of learning wisdom and day-dreaming (see 12:11 and note).

17:25 See verse 21.

17:26 A comment on social wisdom, indicating judicial practices that are corrupt and damage the social order.

17:27 Compare 16:27-28 (see 10:19). The wise man knows how to control his tongue.

17:28 A hypothetical extension of verse 27. Ironically, the fool who has the wit to keep silent shows at least some potential for wisdom.

18:1 The RSV shows something of the difficulty in translating the Hebrew. The NIV is probably correct in suggesting that the unfriendly man (literally "estranged") is self-seeking and acts unwisely.

18:2 Similar to verse 13. *airing his own opinions*. The fool is so full of himself that he has no interest in learning from others; his only desire is to sound off with his own ill-considered ideas.

18:3 The social consequences of folly and wickedness are loss of honour and esteem.

18:4 *deep waters*. Either a natural man's words that are obscure, or a wise man's words that are profound. If the former, then line two contrasts such obscurity with the clarity of wisdom. If the latter, line two develops the theme (the Hebrew has no "but"). This may be a deliberate ambiguity that leaves the application open.

18:5 A judgment on the perversion of justice in which the wicked person is accepted (declared right) and the innocent one is refused vindication.

18:6 See 6:2; 10:11, 14; 13:3; 14:3 and notes.

18:7 See verse 6 and note. *his soul*. His life.

18:8 *like choice morsels*. A comment on sinful human nature: we all have good appetites for gossip.

18:9 See 6:9-11.

18:10 *The name of the Lord*. A covenant proverb which refers to the revealed character of God as the saviour of Israel (see Ex 3:13-15; 15:1-3). The Old Testament presents a contrast between the attempts of sinful humanity to make its own name (reputation) without God (see Gen 11:1-4), and the privilege of the redeemed to be known by the name of the Lord (see Gen 12:1-3; Dt 28:9-10). The people of God are those who shelter in the fortress of God's name; that is, their security is determined by the character of God who declares them to be righteous as he is righteous.

18:11 Contrasts with verse 10. See Luke 12:13-21, but compare 10:15 and note. The implicit warning is against trusting only wealth.

18:12 See 15:33; 16:18-19 and notes.

18:13 By contrast with the wise, the fool will not take the trouble to listen and learn before he blurts out his opinions (see v. 2 and note).

18:14 See 12:25; 15:13; 17:22 and notes.

18:15 See 15:14 and note.

18:16 See 17:8. *A gift*. Not necessarily a bribe, but the practical effects are noted.

18:17 A person's argument in a dispute may be very persuasive until it is challenged by cross-examination or by the other's case. This is a piece of practical wisdom on getting to the truth.

18:18 *the lot*. See 16:33 and note. In Old Testament times before revelation was complete, certain decisions could be made by lot in which it was seen that God controlled the outcome. The lot finds no place in the post-Pentecost church, as Christians today have recourse to the completed canon of Scripture.

18:19 The Hebrew text is obscure. *An offended brother*. The NIV is probably right. (The RSV has "a brother helped.") Because the offended person separates himself from social contact it is hard to approach him and to effect a reconciliation.

18:20 *the fruit of his mouth.* Probably used metaphorically of the constructive aims of wise speech that promotes life-giving relationships.

18:21 By contrast with the wise speech in verse 20, there is also a great potential in words for harm. Because what we say can promote either life or death we should be careful how we speak and what we say.

18:22 See 12:4; 19:14 and notes. *a wife.* There is an assumption here that the wife is a good wife such as in 31:10-31. *favour from the Lord.* See 8:35 where wisdom is similarly described. The favour may mean the blessing of a good wife or the domestic harmony that follows (or both).

18:23 An observation without explicit value judgment on the harsh realities of life in which there are many injustices and inequalities.

18:24 The Hebrew is difficult (see RSV). The contrast seems to be between two kinds of companions. Those whose friendship is superficial will bring us only trouble. But there is a friendship that may go deeper and show more loyalty than that of a brother.

19:1 *Better a poor man.* The poor man who lives a life of integrity is far better off than the perverse man. The implication is that even if the latter is rich he is in reality the loser.

19:2 *zeal without knowledge.* Sincerity and energy are not sufficient if there is no understanding and proper planning in any venture (see Rom 10:2).

19:3 *A man's own folly ruins his life.* Human sinfulness brings misfortune but blames God for it. The person who uses suffering and the mess the world is in as an excuse for unbelief is displaying foolishness.

19:4 See verses 6 and 7. A reality observed without moral judgment.

19:5 See verse 9. In an ordered society perjury is met with stern retribution. False witnesses may flourish in a corrupt society, but where there is social order they will not escape judgment.

19:6 See verses 4 and 7.

19:7 See verses 4 and 6.

19:8 *soul.* Life. Wisdom promotes integrated relationships that are essential for prospering or finding the good life.

19:9 See verse 5 and note.

19:10 *It is not fitting.* The point of this proverb is incongruity. The Hebrew may refer to a fool who is in a position of administrative power rather than one who has wealth. The incongruity of slaves ruling over princes is not so much that the oppressed become the new oppressors, but that they are intellectually and socially unprepared for the complex task of government.

19:11 *patience.* See 14:29; 16:32 and notes. Discipline is a mark of the wise man. Proper self-evaluation prevents him from taking offence at every little insult.

19:12 See 16:14-15 and notes.

19:13 See 10:1 and note; 17:21. Those relationships that are closest and most rewarding have the potential for greater destructiveness. *constant dripping.* Possibly referring to a leaking roof that makes the house uninhabitable during rain (see 27:15).

19:14 There is no suggestion here that God does not have control over inherited wealth. The point is rather that the blessing of a good wife is on an altogether different plane. The outcome of one's choice of spouse is harder to predict or control than material inheritance. Having a happy marriage to a wise woman is cause for grateful thanks to God.

19:15 See 6:9-11; 10:4 and notes.

19:16 See 13:13. *instructions.* Almost certainly a reference to wisdom teaching as in 1:8 and 4:1. *die.* See 2:18 and note.

19:17 The Lord does not leave unrewarded those who show compassion to the poor.

19:18 *discipline.* See 1:2; 3:11 and notes. *hope.* Having reason to expect a desired result. *death.* A life brought to nothing through folly.

19:19 *A hot-tempered man.* Lacking self-control that is a mark of wisdom. He will not learn from his experience, and if you help him out once you will have to do it repeatedly.

19:20 This is an instruction about being wise enough to accept instruction. It is not circular because it points us to the task that carries the content of wisdom (as in 2:1-11).

19:21 See 16:1, 9 and notes.

19:22 The Hebrew is difficult; see the NIV text note. It probably means that a loyal friend, though poor, is better than one who, though he may be rich, is really treacherous.

19:23 *The fear of the Lord.* See 1:7; 2:5 and notes. Probably used here as a synonym for wisdom in which the Lord is the ultimate wise instructor. *life.* See 3:18 and note. *rests content.* Sleeps secure in the care of the Lord.

19:24 *buries his hand in the dish.* Humour is injected here in the portrayal of a person who is so utterly lazy that he cannot even feed himself. The folly lies in the fact that he is not interested in preserving his own life (see 6:6, 10-11).

19:25 *mocker.* See 9:7 and note. He is a person who despises instruction. *simple.* See 1:4 and note. The right relationship between retribution (punishment given because it is deserved) and deterrence is maintained. When the mocker gets what he deserves, the teachable mind of the untutored observes and learns to avoid similar folly. *discerning.* A person who can learn from discipline.

19:26 The self-evident truth of this saying is strengthened by the covenant context that teaches God's purposes for family relationships.

19:28 *corrupt.* Hebrew: *belial*; see note on 6:12; also verse 5.

19:29 See verse 25; 10:13; 14:3. *prepared.* Though the punishment will not deter these fools, it is deserved.

20:1 The second line clarifies the meaning of the first line. *Wine is a mocker.* Either it mocks the person who comes under its spell, or it makes a person become a mocker (see 9:7 and note). *is not wise.* It is foolish to get drunk and/or the drunk is not able to act wisely.

20:2 See 16:14 and note.

20:3 See 15:18 and note.

20:4 *at harvest time.* An obvious example of the wisdom teaching on the appropriate time for various courses of action (see Ecc 3:1-8; Prov 6:6-11).

20:5 *deep waters.* See 18:4 and note. *draws them out.* The wise man can draw wisdom out of obscurity or profundity and make it known.

20:6 Many profess loyalty but few practise it.

20:7 See 13:22 and note, 14:11. *righteous man.* See 8:18 and note. The best kind of father is a righteous one.

20:8 See verse 26. The implication is that the king is wise, as kings should be, and can discern between the wheat and the chaff, that is, between the good and the evil.

20:9 See 16:2. Not so much a theological statement of revelation about original sin as an experience-based recognition of the impossibility of knowing ourselves completely.

20:10 See 11:1; 16:11 and notes.

20:11 *child.* The Hebrew word covers a wide age range from infancy to early adulthood. Even the immature reveal their true character by their behaviour.

20:12 *Ears . . . and eyes.* The two principal means of gaining empirical knowledge are God-given and thus reliable. There may also be an implied warning against the wrong use of them.

20:13 See 6:6-11 and note; 19:15.

20:14 A humorous comment on business strategy. Bargaining was a well-established social ritual in Israel, and this is probably an affirmation of the accepted orderliness of the procedure rather than a rebuke for duplicity.

20:15 See 3:14-15; 8:10-11; 16:16. Wealth is not in itself evil or the mark of folly, but when seen in proper perspective it is less desirable than wisdom.

20:16 *Take the garment.* Taken as security for a loan. *one who puts up security for a stranger.* A person who takes unnecessary financial risks. The meaning seems to be that if you are going to lend to people who are rash in business dealings, you should secure your loans from the beginning.

20:17 The situation referred to in 9:17 is pursued further. *food.* A metaphor for wealth. When wealth is pursued for its own sake, and without a sense of values, it turns sour.

20:18 See 1:5; 15:22. Count the cost and leave nothing to chance.

20:19 See 11:13 and note. Keeping confidence requires the discipline that the gossiper lacks.

20:20 See Exodus 21:17. *his lamp will be snuffed out.* See 13:9 and note. Either by society executing the law, or by divine retribution, or by the natural consequences of such enormous folly.

20:21 *quickly gained at the beginning.* Before one has the wisdom to handle it properly, or perhaps gained by unscrupulous means.

20:22 Although similar to the principle expressed in Deuteronomy 32:35 and Romans 12:19, the wisdom context suggests a more general warning against taking the law into one's own hands and thus undermining the order of society. The deliverance by the Lord is not national (as in Deut 32:35-36) but individual, and therefore is probably through the application of the processes of the law.

20:23 See 16:11 and note; also verse 10.

20:24 See 16:1 and note; 19:21. These are important passages that remind us that human wisdom has limits and must be pursued in the context of the fear of the Lord and the absolute sovereignty of God.

20:25 *dedicate.* Literally "say, 'It is holy.'" The implication is that something is rashly dedicated to God. If the vow cannot be honoured it is worse that no vow at all (see Ecc 5:4-7).

20:26 See verse 8 and note. The wise king can discern the reality behind people's pretences.

20:27 *The lamp of the Lord.* A metaphor for the searching eye of God that can know our inmost thoughts (cf. v. 24).

20:28 *Love and faithfulness.* The same Hebrew words as found in 3:3 (see note). These are usually put together in this way as a covenant term for the faithfulness of God to his promises of salvation. If used here as an empirical wisdom term it probably means the attitude of the king to his people. Thus, his care for his subjects will be reciprocated in social harmony and order. Otherwise the reference may be to God's covenant with the dynasty of David (see 2 Sam 7:11-14).

20:29 See 16:31 and note. While physical strength decreases with age, wisdom increases.

20:30 *Blows and wounds . . . beatings.* Unlike law, wisdom does not prescribe specific punishments for specific offenses. Corporal punishment has a place in prodding the conscience, but it takes wisdom to know when and how to apply it.

21:1 If this refers to kingship in any nation it indicates the sovereignty of God over even those who do not acknowledge him. However, it is more likely that it is a reference to the king of Israel who, like Solomon, receives a special endowment of the wisdom of God.

21:2 See 16:2 and note.

21:3 See verse 27. The prophetic tradition (see 1 Sam 15:22; Isa 1:11-17) has been adapted to the form of a proverb. This kind of statement is rare in the wisdom literature (see 15:8 and note). Nevertheless, the reality expressed is entirely appropriate, for wisdom often contrasts lip-service with integrity.

21:4 *Haughty eyes.* See 6:17. An expression for pride and arrogance similar to "a proud heart." *the lamp.* An obscure metaphor that in 20:27 means the eyes. It may be a repetition of the meaning of the first line, but this is uncertain.

21:5 *The plans of the diligent.* Well thought-out plans diligently carried out are sometimes contrasted with laziness that brings poverty (see v. 25; 19:15). But here the contrast is with rash haste that is just as disastrous as laziness.

21:6 The Hebrew is difficult; see the NIV text note. The meaning is probably similar to that of 20:17.

21:7 *drag them away.* Ensnare them. See 1:18-19 and note; 12:13.

21:8 *upright.* Straight, in the sense of not being devious.

21:9. See also verse 19. *corner of the roof.* Probably a small attic room. *quarrelsome wife.* See 19:13 and note. The quarrelsome wife is the antithesis of the prudent wife in 19:14.

21:10 *evil.* That which destroys human relationships.

21:11 See 19:25 and note.

21:12 *The Righteous One.* While the Hebrew could read "righteous man," it makes better sense if it refers to the Lord. The retribution is then an expression of the righteousness of God.

21:13 *If a man shuts his ears.* The person who lacks a social conscience inevitably cuts himself off from the care of others that he may one day need.

21:14 See 17:8; 18:16 and notes.

21:15 The maintenance of true order (justice) establishes the well-being of those who live according to that order. Those who transgress it will be undone. Wisdom constantly observes the existence of an order that, though marred by sin, is maintained in the world. The assumption is that God preserves the order and that it is our task to perceive it and to live in harmony with it. At its centre is the covenant, and our faithful response to it is what is meant by the fear of the Lord.

21:16 The theme is the contrast of life and death (see 2:18; 3:18 and notes). To forsake wisdom is to forsake life itself and to end up with the dead.

21:17 *wine and oil.* Extravagance, especially in feasting, leads to poverty.

21:18 *ransom.* See 11:8 and note; also Exodus 21:28-30. The ransom was a sum paid to discharge a legal debt. However, this proverb is probably not to be taken in this sense. It is pointing in more general terms to the choice between justification and condemnation. It is unlikely that vicarious suffering for atonement is in view.

21:19 See 19:13; 21:9 and notes.

21:20 Similar to verse 17 but provides the antithesis in the prosperity of the wise.

21:21 The goals and fruits of wisdom are here seen in societal terms. *righteousness.* Right relationships. *love.* Loyalty. *life.* See verse 16 and note.

21:22 See 16:32 and note. Wisdom applied to tactics is superior to mere brute strength. In 2 Corinthians 10:4 the imagery is applied to spiritual warfare. The wisdom of God in the gospel, though it appears to be weak, will always prevail (see 1 Cor 1:25).

21:23 See 13:3; 15:23; 18:13 and notes.

21:24 *"Mocker."* See 9:7; 19:25 and notes.

21:25 See 19:24 and note. The lazy person loses contact with reality and the rewards of hard work.

21:26 This could be a continuation of verse 25; otherwise it contains a contrast between greed and generosity (see 22:9).

21:27 See verse 3; 15:8 and notes.

21:28 See 14:25; 19:5, 9 and notes, but see also the NIV text note.

21:29 *bold front.* Probably bluff and deceit to avoid the consequences of folly. *gives thought to his ways.* The righteous person is prepared to accept the responsibility for his actions.

21:30 No human wisdom is able to stand against God. This not only rebukes the wisdom of sinners but also reminds us that there are limits to even the legitimate empirical wisdom that we seek. The fear of the Lord (see 1:7) puts us in touch with the wisdom of God, but even then there is mystery, as the Book of Job shows.

21:31 Another reflection on the relationship of divine sovereignty and human responsibility. We cannot use trust in God as a means to escape our responsibility. Such wisdom teaching reminds us that the sovereign God has made us responsible for our actions even though he is in control of all things.

22:1 *A good name.* To have a good reputation and to be spoken well of. It is one of the social consequences of wisdom but, as Genesis 11:4 and Luke 6:26 remind us, it can be achieved by wrong methods.

22:2 Every society has its rich and its poor. This is an inescapable fact of human existence over which God the Creator exercises his control. It is also true that the poor are created with the same dignity as the rich. Their value as human beings far outweighs any consideration of wealth.

22:3 Wisdom has great value in teaching us survival in the world. *prudent . . . simple.* See 1:4 and note.

22:4 *Humility and the fear of the Lord.* See 15:33; 1:7 and notes. *wealth and honour and life.* The wise person is able to take control of life in a way the foolish person cannot. The perspective of the empirical wisdom of Proverbs is that wise living usually leads to prosperity. A right relationship with the Lord is the ultimate wisdom that makes for authentic living (see 3:2, 18; 8:18 and notes).

22:5 *thorns and snares.* See 15:19. Metaphors for the reversals of fortune in life which result from a breakdown in the life-giving order. *guards his soul.* Protects his life by seeking to live according to wisdom.

22:6 *Train.* See the NIV text note. The Hebrew carries the idea of inauguration, that is, starting a child's life along a particular way. It is implied that this way is the way of wisdom. True wisdom will maintain itself through the whole of life because it involves the humility to go on seeking more wisdom.

22:7 Compare 10:15 and note. This is a simple observation of a social fact: wealth is power.

22:8 Folly is the transgression of true, life-giving relationships and so in the end it brings self-destruction (see Hos 8:7; Gal 6:7-9).

22:9 *A generous man.* Literally "a good eye." One who is well disposed to those around him. His own well-being is bound up with that of others so that what he does for their good rebounds onto himself (see 19:17).

22:10 *mocker.* See 9:7 and note. Social harmony cannot exist with such a person stirring up strife.

22:11 See 8:15; 14:35; 16:12-13; 20:26 and notes. The assumption is that the king is Israel's. He is ideally the true representative of wisdom from God.

22:12 *the eyes of the Lord.* See 15:3; 20:8, 27 and notes. A theological observation rather than an empirical one. God prospers his truth as he works his purposes out.

22:13 *The sluggard.* See 6:6 and note. With humour and irony, the proverb mocks the lazy person's excuse-making to avoid going to work.

22:14 See 5:3-5; 6:24; 7:5, 14-21. Here the fool's downfall through his own folly is seen as due to the wrath of God.

22:15 *Folly is bound up in the heart of a child.* Although not a theological statement on original or inborn sin, experience supports this notion. *the rod of discipline.* It is not clear that this refers to corporal punishment, although the text could bear this meaning. The rod may be metaphorical (though see 13:24; 29:15). Discipline is the educational function of wisdom, thus, instruction in wisdom may be like a rod in driving out folly.

22:16 There are some ambiguities in the Hebrew text. The NIV supplies "both" thus applying poverty to each person alike. It may, however, be a contrast between riches gained through oppression and poverty suffered through a vain attempt to buy favour from a rich man. Thus, experience shows that one is more easily able to get money from the poor than from the rich.

7

More instructions Proverbs 22:17-24:34

Common wisdom and distinctive wisdom

Scholars have long been fascinated by the sayings in Proverbs 22:17-23:11 because they raise the question of a possible common cross-cultural pool of wisdom in the Ancient Near East. There is nothing in the material as such that suggests anything other than an Israelite origin, but when close parallels were discovered to exist between this part of Proverbs and some Egyptian wisdom literature the matter was opened up. The weight of opinion now seems to favour the notion that an Egyptian wise man, Amen-em-ope, was responsible for the older material, and that an Israelite wise man adapted it for his own use. However, this opinion is not without its critics who suggest that the evidence for such a relationship is slim.

The idea that some pagan literature could have been worked into the Bible is difficult for some Christians to swallow. The matter might be ignored since there is no reference to such a pagan origin in the text. Not so easy to ignore, however, are the words that are explicitly attributed to Agur (Prov 30:1) and Lemuel (Prov 31:1). These men do not appear to be Israelites. Were they converts to the faith of Israel? Have their writings been "baptised" through a process of modification to an Israelite way of thinking? Or is there a legitimate area of common wisdom that is valid for all people? Certainly the comparison of Solomon's wisdom with that of pagans (see I Ki 4:29-34) and his ability to make meaningful contact with the pagan Queen of Sheba's wisdom (see 1 Ki 10:1-6) show some common ground.

An illustration may help us to appreciate the distinctives of Israelite wisdom within a common human wisdom. Much wisdom, as we have seen, operates at the everyday and practical level. In modern society the law says, in effect, "You shall not drive through a red traffic light." Wisdom would make an observation such as, "The wise person stops at red lights and thus avoids injury in a collision." Or it might put it negatively, thus: "The fool ignores the red light and so brings himself and the innocent to destruction." One does not have to be a Christian to accept the common wisdom of these two statements. Christian, Jewish, Muslim, pagan and atheistic societies would all agree on the validity of this wisdom. A modern book of Proverbs might easily contain similar observations borrowed from non-Israelite or non-Christian contexts. The distinctions between the different kinds of wisdom will become obvious only when the situations are viewed in the context of ultimate reality. Thus the Christian might go on from the simple observation of the likely effect of ignoring traffic lights to reflect on why it is so. He or she might consider matters of velocity, braking capabilities of the family car, the fragility of the human body in a high speed impact, and so on. But eventually the moral and spiritual dimensions would enter. Human sin and responsibility are factors that a Christian will have distinct views on. Why things are what they are can only be resolved in ultimate terms when the revelation of God is appealed to.

In the end, facts are facts only because God is the Creator and establishes the meaning of all circumstances.

More specifically, Amen-em-ope is not a threat to the Bible as the inspired word of God. First, this is so because inspiration does not preclude an inspired author borrowing someone else's material. Rather, divine inspiration is the guarantee that, whatever the source, the words of the Bible say what God wants them to say. Secondly, the common store of human wisdom contains much that is written at the practical level of behaviour without ever raising the question of eternal significance. Thirdly, such wisdom incorporated into the inspired body of Scripture is important for giving us the correct perspective on the way we, as Christians, go about the task of gathering knowledge. Rather than degrading Scripture the use of common wisdom shows that all true knowledge must have a theological dimension behind it, even if this is not explicitly stated. It also shows that secular statements are not necessarily wrong as far as they go, but that they are limited in that they cannot bring us to ultimate truth. As always, we are driven back to the principle of the fear of the Lord as that which renews the Christian's mind and enables us to view all facts in the light of God's self-revelation.

It is imperative that we recognise the significance of Jesus Christ as "the truth" (Jn 14:6). As we read and contemplate the wise sayings in this section we need to remember the principles we have already discussed for making legitimate Christian contact with what the ancient Israelite wisdom says. Whenever the old wisdom seems to speak immediately to our own modern experience we will no doubt feel a sense of the relevance of the material. But we must not lose sight of the fact that these writings are part of the sacred Scripture which testifies to Christ (see Jn 5:39; Lk 24:27, 44-45). It would be a mistake to concentrate on the wisdom sayings as examples for living and useful knowledge (which they undoubtedly are) but fail to see how they testify to Christ. For in the end we need to realise that our Christian lives are lived not by becoming exceedingly canny and shrewd, but by faith in Christ. Our wisdom is above all things found in the gospel: Christ is our wisdom. The gift of God to us through the gospel is the status of the perfectly wise person because Christ is the Wise Man *for us*. The task we have as Christians is to translate this truth into daily living, and that is where the experiences of the wise men of old are still valuable.

Comments on Proverbs 22:17-24:34

22:17-21 This introductory section calls the pupil to be attentive to the teachings of the wise man. It also shows the benefits of learning wisdom.

22:17 *apply your heart.* Think carefully (see 2:1-2 and notes).

22:18 *heart.* Literally "inmost part" (see 18:8). *ready on your lips.* Learned so that they are ready for application.

22:19 *trust . . . in the Lord.* A clear sign of the thoroughly Israelite outlook on wisdom, whether or not some material is borrowed (see 3:5 and note).

22:20 *thirty sayings.* See the NIV text note. The first reading is preferred because the section divides into roughly thirty parts, and because Amen-em-ope wrote thirty chapters (see introduction to this section).

22:21 *to him who sent you.* Probably the wisdom teacher. This may reflect the role of wisdom instruction in training diplomats.

22:22-23 A short instructional piece with divine retribution as the motive. The Lord is pictured as the one who is the ultimate legal-aid attorney, defending the poor who are oppressed even in the law courts.

22:24-25 *Do not make friends.* Unwise friendships are the subject of a number of sayings (e.g. 1:10-19; 12:26). *a hot-tempered man.* One who is quick to lose self-control (see 14:17, 29; 15:18 and notes).

22:26-27 See 6:1-5 and notes.

22:28 See 15:25 and notes. In 23:10-11 the matter is given theological motivation. Here there is no motive clause and the thought behind it may be social order that is undermined by such injustice.

22:29 *skilled.* Literally "quick." The man's speed comes from his well-learned skills rather than from taking short-cuts. *he will serve before kings.* An indirect exhortation to excellence that, in the Egyptian schools of the wise, was the way of promotion in an elite civil service. If this thought has an Egyptian origin it is still appropriate in its Israelite setting.

23:1-3 An instruction that links a person's table manners with character and probably with ability as a diplomat. The training of such officials was a principal aim in Egyptian wisdom.

23:1-2 *note well what is before you.* See the NIV text note. Either, "do not allow the feast to excite you with greed" or, "pay attention to the great man and not to the food." *put a knife to your throat.* Take whatever measures are needed to curb your tendency to gluttony.

23:3 *that food is deceptive.* Gluttony will destroy human relationships and their advantages.

23:4-5 The perspective of wisdom recognises the greater values in life. It is not worth ruining one's health for riches that have the habit of disappearing the moment you take your eyes off them.

23:6 *a stingy man.* The meaning of the Hebrew is uncertain. The context suggests a man who is insincere in his hospitality, presumably for ulterior motives.

23:8 *vomit.* A metaphor for a spoiled relationship and the feeling of disgust at someone's insincerity.

23:9 An unusually short instruction containing a command and a single motive clause. It thus has more the force of a proverbial sentence, echoing the teaching of 9:7 and other proverbs that show how unteachable fools are.

23:10-11 See 15:25; 22:28 and notes.

23:11 *Defender.* Literally "redeemer" (see RSV); one who accepted the role of a family member or relative in helping a person in need (see Lev 25:25; Ruth 3:12-13). The RSV and NIV capitalise the word to show that God is the redeemer who defends and saves his people (see Job 19:25; Ps 19:14; Is 41:14; 43:14; 44:24).

23:13-14 An instruction on parental discipline (see 13:24; 19:18; 22:6, 15 and notes).

23:13 *he will not die.* Either "it will not unduly hurt him" or "he will avoid death" (which is the meaning of v. 14).

23:14 *death*. Hebrew: *sheol* (see 1:12; 2:18 and notes).

23:15-16 The actual instruction (to seek wisdom) is implied in the motive. The latter shows that in human relationships true wisdom is not a cold and merely intellectual thing; it strengthens right relationships and brings joy.

23:17-18 This instruction is given explicitly in the framework of the covenant and the promises of God. It is another reminder of the limitations of wisdom based on experience. There are many situations in life, including suffering, when God's people are thrown onto the revealed goodness of God. Trust in his word is the basis of hope.

23:17 *the fear of the Lord*. See 1:7 and note.

23:18 *future hope . . . your hope*. An unusual perspective in wisdom but probably a hope for life after death.

23:19-21. *keep your heart on the right path*. An instruction on following wisdom. The references to poor company, drunkenness and gluttony are examples of the foolish life that easily overtakes a person.

23:22-25 An instruction to children on harmonious and joyful family relationships established on wisdom. While pointing in the same direction as the fifth commandment (see Ex 20:12), it is based not directly on the divine law but on the discerning observation of human relationships (see vv. 15-16 and note).

23:26-28 An instruction that warns against immorality (see 2:16-19; 5:1-20).

23:26 *give me your heart.* In other words, "Pay attention! Give your mind to what I say" (see note on 2:2). The wisdom teacher exhorts the pupil to trust his teaching.

23:27 *deep pit.* A pit to trap wild animals. *wayward wife.* Literally "a foreign woman," therefore one who is not an adherent of the covenant law of Israel. The term is used for immoral or adulterous persons (see 2:16 and note). *narrow well.* One from which it is impossible to escape.

23:28 *unfaithful.* Unfaithful in marriage.

23:29-35 The perils of drunkenness are put as a riddle. The effects are described, first, as others see the drunkard (v. 29) and secondly, as the drunkard experiences the results of his folly (vv. 33-35). Here is a negation of all the personal qualities that wisdom recommends: self-control, clear perception of reality, and positive relationships.

23:30 *mixed wine.* See 9:2 and note.

23:31 *Do not gaze at the wine when it is red.* Probably a reference to being so fascinated by the colour so that caution is discarded.

23:32 *In the end it bites like a viper.* The aftermath of heavy drinking, a strong hangover, is as debilitating as a snake bite.

23:33 *strange sights . . . confusing things.* Hallucinations and muddled thinking.

23:34 *like one sleeping on the high seas.* Lying down will not stop the feeling of dizziness. *lying on top of the rigging.* The meaning is not certain, though the phrase suggests a terrible sense of instability.

23:35 *but I'm not hurt.* The person so besotted by wine that he cannot perceive his injuries. *so I can find another drink.* The alcoholic craves more, despite the pain it has already brought him. Addiction is the loss of control over one's life.

24:1-2 See 23:17-18 and notes; 24:19. *their hearts plot violence.* These are not witless fools, but evil people who use all their intellectual powers to take advantage of others.

24:3-4 *wisdom . . . understanding . . . knowledge.* Synonyms. *a house.* Conceivably a literal dwelling because wisdom is used in the Old Testament to mean the skill of craftsmen and builders (e.g. Ex 36:1). *rare and beautiful treasures.* These would then be the wealth gained through wisdom. But "house" can also mean a family (as in "household") or dynasty (e.g. 2 Sam 7:11-12). In this case the treasures would be the wealth of human relationships as well as legitimately achieved prosperity.

24:5-6 See 11:14; 21:22 and notes.

24:7 *too high.* Wisdom is out of the fool's reach since he is unteachable. *the gate.* In Israelite society the traditional meeting place for counsel and judgment was the town gate.

24:8 *will be known as a schemer.* Reputation in any society carries great weight. The prospect of being known as anti-social can be a strong deterrent against evil-doing.

24:9 *The schemes of folly are sin.* It is possible that this saying is a unit with verse 8. Folly here is not a light thing; it is seen as rebellion against the order which God has established in his revelation. There is also the social sanction of being detested by society.

24:10 *in times of trouble.* A person's emotional and moral strength is only revealed when it is truly tested.

24:11-12 These two verses are best taken together. We cannot use the excuse of ignorance to avoid the responsibility to help another in need. *he who weighs the heart.* God watches over the interests of the needy and perceives our failures to act to help them.

24:13-14. The metaphor in verse 14 depends on the literal meaning of verse 13. *wisdom is sweet to your soul.* Good food nourishes the body, and in the same way wisdom nourishes the inner life. *future hope.* See 23:17-18 and note.

24:15-16 The assumption is that God does not allow the unrighteous to prosper permanently. While the righteous may suffer many adversities, God will finally vindicate them.

24:17-18 *Do not gloat.* On its own this direction would make perfect sense as implying that compassion cannot be entirely withdrawn from any other human being even when that person is an enemy. The problem is the apparently contradictory motive given in verse 18 that implies that our gloating lets the enemy off the hook. Perhaps the meaning is that the person who is without kindness towards an enemy is even more deserving of God's wrath.

24:19-20 *Do not fret.* Literally "become hot;" that is, do not become agitated. *or be envious.* See verse 1. *future hope.* See 23:18 and note.

24:21-22. *Fear the Lord.* See 1:7 and note. *and the king.* In Israel's covenant-based society the king became the exemplar of wisdom and the agent of God's wise rule. *will send sudden destruction.* Righteous retribution from the Lord may come directly or through his appointed agent the king; it is necessary for the existence of a just society and for the maintenance of order and truth.

24:23-34 *These also are sayings of the wise.* It would appear that these sayings have been inserted here by an editor because their form is closer to the instructions which precede them than to the sentence literature which follows.

24:23b-25 Justice in the social context is important. Wisdom promotes a well-ordered society in which justice is both done and seen to be done.

24:26 *like a kiss on the lips.* The most intimate expression of friendship. Honesty and friendship belong together.

24:27 *build your house.* Either (or both) build your dwelling or establish your family (see vv. 3-4 and note). Both tasks need a firm economic basis before they are undertaken.

24:28-29 These two verses seem to belong together. Thus, there are two related situations to avoid: one is the giving of false witness against another (see 6:16, 19); the other is the taking of revenge born of the heat of passion. Such loss of self-control is not the way of wisdom.

24:30-34 This should be read together with 6:6-11 (see with notes). There the consideration of the ant as an object lesson leads to the proverbial saying in verses 10-11. In the present passage the same proverb is applied to the observation of the lazy man's vineyard. This suggests something of the openness of application of proverbial sayings. Here the folly of the lazy farmer combines with the forces of natural disorder in a fallen world. Such poverty born of folly is as destructive as the social disorder caused by thieves.

8

Wisdom from Hezekiah's wise men Proverbs 25:1-29:27

Comments on Proverbs 25:1-29:27

25:1 *more proverbs of Solomon.* See notes on 1:1 and chapter 4: "By whom and when?" *copied.* It is likely that the centralised administration set up by David resulted in professional writers or scribes being employed. The Hebrew word used here means "transmission" and may refer to the committing of oral tradition to writing, or to copying and editing something already written. *Hezekiah.* King of Judah at the time of the destruction of the northern kingdom of Israel (722 B.C.). He promoted reform of the many corrupt religious practices in Judah. The destruction of Israel did not have much effect on the people of Judah in motivating them to avoid the same fate that the prophets said would be the divine response to faithlessness. This reference to Hezekiah shows that he was concerned not only to return to the covenant law of Moses but also to encourage the literary activity of the wisdom movement.

25:2 *the glory of God.* Includes his sovereign will that he does not reveal. This mystery in God involves not only what is beyond human understanding but also that which God conceals from us so that we might respond to him in trust and with awe and reverence. On the other hand, the king in Israel was to reflect God's rule to the people (see 16:12-15; 20:8, 26; 25:3, 5; Dt 17:18-20), though he is still human and must also submit to the fact of mystery in God's sovereign will. Thus, the king also reflects the human response to God in fidelity to the law and in the quest for knowledge and wisdom.

25:3 *unsearchable.* When the king exemplifies human wisdom his mind is not an open book to others. It is possible that this saying reflects the importance given to training in wisdom for the nobility and especially for those in the royal succession.

25:4-5 *Remove the dross.* No matter how skilled the craftsman is, he must always have good materials to work with. In the same way, the king needs a society purged of evil elements if he is to establish a righteous rule. Good order in society cannot be simply commanded from the throne.

25:6-7 The wisdom of the royal court observes an unspoken protocol. It rebukes conceit and self-seeking that can overreach itself and lead to humiliation; it is better to start out with humility and then be exalted. Jesus adapted this instruction in the parable of Luke 14:7-11 to apply to the place of his followers in the kingdom of God.

25:7c-8 The Hebrew text is followed by the KJV which places the last part of verse 7 with what goes before. The NIV and RSV agree with the many other versions that place it with verse 8. *court.* Either in legal dispute or in government. The principle is to be careful before testifying against your neighbour lest the process backfire on you. It is probably aimed at those who have a propensity to intervene in other people's disputes rather than at those who do their duty in pursuit of justice.

25:9-10 This instruction is concerned with the betrayal of confidences. A third party is involved in a dispute that is not his. When the matter goes badly, this person is unnecessarily harmed and the first party gains a reputation for disloyalty which is hard to shake off.

25:11 The Hebrew lacks the words "is like" in the second line. It reads literally, "Apples of gold in settings of silver, a word aptly spoken." This kind of comparison (see also vv. 12, 13, 14, 18, 20, 25, 26, 28) simply places two or more things side by side, leaving us to work out the nature of the comparison and why these things go together. It is not at all clear that the translators are accurate in supplying "is like" which ties us to one kind of comparison. When we use the form "a is like b" we imply that "b" is known and that its attributes can be transferred to the "a" that is not known. But when these proverbs place "a" next to "b" it is left open as to which item is regarded as known. It is possible that the intention of the writer is to say, "These things belong together, and it takes wisdom to see why." Thus, this kind of saying is more an exercise in discerning order and relationships than an informative simile. In verse 11 well-chosen words share a wisely discernible property with fine craftsmanship.

25:12 *an ear-ring . . . an ornament.* Two pieces of complementary jewellery (the Hebrew links them with "and"), and a good relationship between the wise man and his receptive pupil are somehow alike. Thus, either a rebuke is valuable like gold, or a wise rebuke complements a receptive ear as one piece of jewellery complements another.

25:13 The imagery is curious. Snow at harvest would normally be disastrous but, as in verse 25, it is its refreshing quality that is in mind. The third line shows that someone saw the need to clarify this point.

25:14 *Like clouds . . without rain.* See Jude 12. Palestinians experienced all too often clouds that promised much-needed rain only to disappoint. Today we might apply this to those who seek power and influence, whether political or personal, by making promises without substance.

25:15 A word for diplomats but relevant to others: even great and influential people can be persuaded when we avoid anger and resist provocation. *break a bone.* A metaphor for the breaking of resistance.

25:16-17 Two separate sayings probably placed together because they have the same message about knowing when to stop. *honey.* It is good to eat, but too much will make a person sick. This proverb is open to all kinds of applications beyond that of food. Likewise, neighbourly friendship is good, but too much running next door becomes an abuse of the other's privacy. It takes wisdom to perceive rightly how a relationship should be defined when there are no written rules.

25:18 *club . . sword . . arrow.* Weapons of war and false testimony belong in the same category; they are all lethal means of assaulting another person.

25:20 Comparison of the RSV, NIV and KJV shows some problem with the Hebrew text. The form of this proverb invites us to understand what these three situations have in common. The RSV follows the Greek Old Testament and reads "wound" for the NIV's "soda." The common feature may be provocation, or it may be some self-inflicted hurt. *sings songs to a heavy heart.* The Hebrew allows "on" or "with" a heavy heart (as in Ps 137:3-4).

25:21-22 *you will heap burning coals on his head.* The origin of this metaphor is obscure and its significance can only be guessed at from the context. Psalm 140:10 suggests punishment, and Paul in Romans 12:20 sees it as overcoming evil with good, but he does not explain. The most likely meaning is penitence through a burning sense of shame. Some argue an Egyptian origin in a penitential rite in which coals were carried on the head to show contrition. This instruction may have originated as wisdom based on experience, but it is here placed in the framework of a covenantal word. Apart from Exodus 23:4-5 there is little by way of kindness to enemies enjoined on Israel. This is probably because of the theological significance of the enemies as those who oppose God's kingdom and the salvation of Israel. Jesus expressed the related implications of the gospel in Matthew 5:43-48.

25:23 *As a north wind brings rain.* This climatic detail is only important because it expresses an inevitable relationship of cause and effect.

25:24 See 21:9 and note.

25:25 For the form of this proverb see the notes for verses 11 and 12. *soul.* That the whole person is indicated is clear from the fact that water refreshes it. Hebrew thought does not conceive of humans as souls (spirits) in physical bodies, but as bodies animated by spirit. "Soul" often means the whole person.

25:26 The form is the same as verse 25. The common feature in the three elements is the corruption of character. Springs, wells and righteous people should all sustain life, and it is a terrible contradiction when they fail to do so.

25:27 *honey.* See verses 16 and 17 and note. The Hebrew of line two is difficult. The NIV solves the problem by adding "nor," though the connection between the two parts is still obscure.

25:28 The form is the same as verse 25. The Hebrew leaves it open as to what is being compared to what by simply indicating that the two elements go together. We are thus challenged not merely to learn another proverb, but to discern the common factor establishing an otherwise unobserved relationship. In this case it is probably vulnerability to attack.

26:1 This is an unambiguous comparison as the Hebrew has "like . . . so." The perceptible order in nature cannot be reversed without serious consequences. The incongruity of unseasonable weather illustrates that of honouring the fool.

26:2 The form is the same as verse 1. There is a similarity in purpose to the common proverb, "Sticks and stones will break my bones, but names will never hurt me." Curses have no magical power to inflict harm on the innocent. If it is deserved it is an expression of the appropriate retribution. Otherwise it is empty and cannot "come to rest," that is, stick.

26:3 It is interesting that the form of this proverb is the same as 25:20 and the other sayings for which the translators have provided "like . . . is." *horse . . . donkey . . . the backs of fools.* The common feature here is coercion as the only way to get through to such creatures. The fool is thus seen in the company of brute beasts and as not having the dignity of a reasoning being.

26:4-5 These two sayings should be taken together. They display the important principle that proverbs are not timeless general rules. The apparent contradiction involved is resolved when we realise that proverbs are usually based on observations of specific events. Thus, one situation is best handled by refusing to play the fool's game with him, while another demands some rejoinder to his folly. Life is full of both kinds of situations, and these two sayings remind us that there is no one clear-cut response. One must assess each situation carefully and decide whether to engage the fool or disengage from his company.

26:6 Compare the RSV and NIV translations. Again there is the note of incongruity. The diplomatic scene may well be in view but there are wider applications. An important message is as effective as the one to whom it is entrusted. Sending a fool on the errand is like being legless, that is, like being without any messenger at all. *drinking violence.* Suffering violence, but compare this with 4:17 where the meaning is different.

26:7 *Like a lame man's legs that hang limp.* A wisdom saying uttered by a fool is so incongruous with his life that is loses all its power.

26:8 The form is the same as verse 1. The absurdity of tying the stone in the sling so that it cannot be slung illustrates the absurdity of honouring a fool.

26:9 *Like a thorn bush in a drunkard's hand.* The Hebrew is unclear. Perhaps it refers to a thorn piercing a man's hand while he is too drunk to even be aware of it, but how a proverb in the fool's mouth is similar is not clear. Another suggestion is that the saying envisages a drunk who has torn a branch from a tree and is wielding it in a comical or absurd way. So the fool is a figure of derision as he attempts to handle wise sayings.

26:10 Again the Hebrew is difficult. It possibly refers to the reckless abandonment of any sound judgment or the use of reason.

26:11 Unlike the simple but teachable person (see 1:4 and note), the fool will not learn from his mistakes but rather returns, like a dog to its vomit, to repeat them. It is interesting that, as any dog-owner will know, the dog's habit is usually beneficial to itself. Thus, the force of the comparison depends on the distaste that humans naturally have for the idea.

26:12 *a man wise in his own eyes.* There are degrees of folly, and the most extreme is seen in the fool who is so far gone that he cannot perceive his own folly. Another extreme example is seen in the foolishness of sinful humanity that sees itself as wiser than the wisdom of God (see 1 Cor 1:18-2:5).

26:13-16 Here is a group of four proverbs that reflect on laziness. In this fallen world humans must work hard to win sustenance from the earth. It is folly to ignore this fact of human existence, and laziness works against a well-ordered human life. See also 6:6-11; 24:30-34 and notes.

26:13 See 22:13 and note.

26:14 *As a door turns on its hinges.* The behaviour of the lazy person puts him on the same level of existence as an inanimate object. Humorously this proverb suggests that there is no more difference between the sluggard and his bed than between a door and its hinge.

26:15 See 19:24 and note.

26:16 *wiser in his own eyes.* A lazy person is bound to lose contact with the real world. He feeds his self-delusion that he is in total control of his life, something that the wise are not willing to claim for themselves.

26:17 *Like one who seizes a dog by the ears.* Anyone who has grabbed a strange dog by the ears will know the force of this saying! It is not clear in the Hebrew if the "passer-by" refers to the dog or the meddler. If the former, the emphasis is on unprovoked interference. If the latter, it would emphasise the folly of getting involved in disputes about which we know nothing.

26:18-19 *a madman shooting . . . a man who deceives his neighbour.* The common element is the potential for destruction; the first (v. 18) to property and persons, and the second (v. 19) to personal relationships.

26:20 *without gossip a quarrel dies down.* The gossip engages in malicious talk with little concern for truth. Remove this element and many quarrels die through lack of fuel.

26:21 Similar to verse 20. *As charcoal to embers.* The quarrelsome person is one who cannot resist undermining personal relationships by introducing contention into them.

26:22 See 18:8 and note.

26:23 *Like a coating of glaze.* See the NIV text note. The Hebrew text is difficult and the point of the comparison obscure. The NIV and RSV (cf. KJV) suggest that the meaning is a pleasing veneer that hides the real nature underneath.

26:24 The meaning is the same as verse 23.

26:25-26 *do not believe him.* The man of verse 24 must be avoided. *his wickedness will be exposed.* In time people will see through his deceptions.

26:27 *If a man digs a pit, he will fall into it.* The trouble-maker makes trouble for himself. This theme of retribution is probably intended to be linked with verses 23 to 26. Here the emphasis is not on divine judgment but on the self-destructive nature of folly aimed at destroying others.

26:28 Hatred is the ultimate breakdown of human relationships (see 1 Jn 3:15). Human speech has enormous potential for evil and its misuse cannot be lightly excused (see Jas 3:5-10). *a flattering mouth.* Literally "a smooth talker." Here it is the same as the lying tongue.

27:1 *you do not know.* The wise will understand the limits of human wisdom. Being prepared by planning for the future does not mean that we can have complete control of it. The fool may think he is control but he does not reckon on the sovereign will of God (see Lk 12:19-20; Jas 4:13-15).

27:2 *Let another praise you.* Wisdom includes humility.

27:3-4 *Stone . . . sand.* Two comparisons that emphasise the destructiveness of folly.

27:5 *Better is open rebuke.* A salutary word spoken for correction is better than misguided love that lacks the moral strength to risk a rebuke.

27:6 *Wounds from a friend.* Similar to the "open rebuke" in verse 5. *multiplies kisses.* Unlike the love in verse 5, this is a sham.

27:7 See 25:16, 27 and notes. *hungry . . . tastes.* The meaning of the proverb is not limited to food but applies to anything for which we have an appetite.

27:8 *Like a bird that strays.* The importance of human relationships is seen when a wanderer deprives himself and others of such bonds.

27:9 The Hebrew is difficult (compare NIV with RSV). The NIV follows the Hebrew more closely. *joy to the heart.* The emphasis is on the benefits of a close personal relationship.

27:10 *better a neighbour nearby.* The point of this instruction seems to be that we should develop relationships beyond the immediate family, for sometimes a brother will not, or cannot, come to our aid.

27:11 See 10:1. This is not mere self-interest but a recognition of the importance of testing our work by the good effect it has on others.

27:12 *The prudent.* See 1:4; 12:16 and notes. *the simple.* See note on 1:4. These are the untutored, and the emphasis is on being taught wisdom.

27:13 See 20:16 and note.

27:14 See 26:18-19, 24-26. *If a man loudly blesses his neighbour.* Probably a reference to false and inappropriately timed protestations of friendship that cloak an evil intent.

27:15-16 See 19:13 and note. *restraining . . . grasping.* It is almost impossible to control a quarrelsome wife.

27:17 The exact meaning of the second part of this saying is not obvious (literally "sharpens his neighbour's face"), but it probably refers to a man's intellectual powers and their effect on character.

27:18 See 22:29. Diligent work and honest service are rewarded.

27:19 The sparing use of words in the Hebrew leaves both the translation and interpretation open to a certain amount of guess-work. Assuming the NIV is accurate, the sense is still obscure because we usually think of one's words and actions as reflecting one's thoughts or heart (see Mt 7:20; 15:18); here the reverse seems to be indicated. The first line suggests that by looking at others we see ourselves reflected; we know ourselves only by looking at others. Another possibility is that our thoughts, as they are expressed in action, reflect our character.

27:20 *Death and Destruction are never satisfied.* See 15:11 and note. The parallel with destruction suggests that the insatiability of the eyes means the awakening of endless desires which threaten our well-being.

27:21 Compare 17:3. *man is tested by the praise he receives.* How we handle praise is an indicator of wisdom and moral strength; learning to handle it without giving in to pride is a refining experience.

27:22 *mortar.* A sturdy bowl for grinding substances in. *pestle.* A club-shaped grinding tool. This proverb sees the fool as unteachable even when the most extreme measures are used.

27:23-27 This group of sayings expresses a concern for care of the resources upon which life depends. Sustainable resources carefully used are more to be desired than riches that are easily dissipated. The wisdom theme is the careful attention to the order of things so that life is supported. The ecological implications of these sayings are more obvious in our age in which the very existence of the planet is under threat.

28:1 Because of the greater attention to theological matters in the sayings of chapter 28 we must reckon on the possibility that some, such as verse 1, are reflections on the righteousness of God rather than on human experience. Thus, the wicked feel insecure because of their deeds. The righteous are secure because they are vindicated by their relationship to God.

28:2 The difficulty of the Hebrew text is reflected in the way the Greek version reinterprets it, and is followed by the NEB. The KJV, RSV and NIV are largely in agreement that the meaning is that unrighteousness and political instability, as in the northern kingdom of Israel, go hand in hand, while a wise or righteous man maintains social order.

28:3 The problem in the text is indicated by the NIV text note. A single vowel change gives "head man" or "ruler" which the NIV follows (cf. RSV: "poor man"). Both rain and a ruler have the potential for great good or great evil.

28:4 *law.* Probably the law of Moses since this was the basis of Israelite society. Although wisdom tends to reflect more on human experience than on God's revelation, the wise men were still men of the covenant who were concerned for the law and its demands.

28:5 *justice.* Either God's moral rule of the universe, or the good order of things of which God's rule is the presupposition. Justice is not something that can be intuitively understood. What we call natural justice often goes astray since it does not draw its principles from God's revelation. *those who seek the Lord.* Those whose faith recognises the subordination of all things to the sovereignty of God. *understand it fully.* This does not mean having total knowledge or being infallible; rather it reflects the fear of the Lord as the key to understanding ultimate truth, and foreshadows the fact that Jesus Christ is the truth.

28:6 See also verse 11. *blameless.* See 2:7 and note. Human relationships and a person's relationship to God are more important than riches.

28:7 *law.* Either wisdom instruction or the law of Moses (or both). See verse 4 and note; 23:19-25 and notes.

28:8 In Leviticus 25:35-38 the principle is established on the basis of the grace of God that we should help others freely and not for gain (see also Dt 23:19-20). *amasses it for another.* The justice of God will not allow the greedy rich to hold on to their wealth. As a principle this may seem to be contradicted by the fact of the prosperous wicked. In the Old Testament there was a general correlation observed that is sometimes contravened; the New Testament reminds us that God's justice is ultimately worked out.

28:9 See 15:8, 29. *law.* See verse 4 and note. Most probably the revealed law of God. *prayers.* This connection lies in the fact that prayer is a response to God's revelation in his word; when prayer ignores and even despises God's word it is not acceptable to God. The New Testament develops this theme to show that our prayer is acceptable only through Christ who is our mediator (see Jn 14:13-14).

28:10 See 26:27. *blameless.* One who fears the Lord. The justice of God seems to be implied here; there is a special judgment on those who seek to seduce God's people (see Mt 5:19; 18:6).

28:11 See verse 6. While having riches does not necessarily correlate with unrighteousness, nor poverty with wisdom and righteousness, there is that tendency nevertheless (see vv. 6, 8, 20, 22, 25, 27). *wise in his own eyes.* See 26:5, 16. There is no greater fool than the one who thinks of his folly as wisdom (cf. 1 Cor 1:18-25).

28:12 See verse 28; 29:2. Righteousness means social order and happiness, while unrighteousness destroys and alienates.

28:13 See Psalm 32:1-4; 1 John 1:6-9. Order and well-being in one's life, the chief concerns of wisdom, are here linked with one's personal relationship to God. Sin breaks that relationship, and to leave it unconfessed and not dealt with is the ultimate disorder of life. It is basic to the theology of the Bible that all relationships depend on the nature of our relationship to God.

28:14 *Blessed.* See 3:13 and note. *fears the Lord.* See 1:7 and note. *hardens his heart.* Sets one's will against the Lord (see Ex 7:3, 13). *falls into trouble.* Because his life lacks the true basis of order and prosperity.

28:15 See verses 3 and 16.

28:16 *A tyrannical ruler.* Tyranny is so contrary to wisdom that it shows a lack of discernment. The implication in the second line is that the greedy tyrant causes his own destruction.

28:17 *A man tormented by the guilt of murder.* The murderer cannot escape, nor be helped to escape, the inevitable judgment of God.

28:18 See verses 13 and 14; 10:9 and note.

28:19 See 12:11 and note.

28:20 Faith and wisdom come before riches, but riches without faith lead a person astray.

28:21 See 18:5; 24:23. Even a small bribe can cause disastrous results to the maintenance of order and justice in society.

28:22 See verse 20b. *A stingy man.* See 23:6 and note. *poverty awaits him.* Either the stingy man lacks the wisdom to gain and to keep wealth, or God's justice will not allow him to be rich.

28:23 See 27:5. People generally are not fooled by flattery and will treat it with the disdain it deserves. On the other hand, a needed rebuke can have a positive effect on personal relationships.

28:24 See 19:26 and note. *"It's not wrong."* Family relationships are at the centre of all human bonds. To rob one's parents without any shame shows a moral depravity that is destructive in the extreme.

28:25 *stirs up dissension.* See 6:13-14. Greed leads to the kind of disorder in life which makes it impossible to prosper. *trusts the Lord.* Trust is not inactivity but harmony with God and his ways. Reliance and faith are the same as the fear of the Lord (see 1:7 and note).

28:26 Compare verse 25 where trusting in the Lord is wisdom. *trusts in himself.* See 3:5-6 and notes. Trust in self is the destructive opposite of trusting the Lord. *walks in wisdom.* Trusts the Lord.

28:27 See 11:24-26; 14:21; 22:9 and notes. *receives many curses.* Either the results of an anti-social life, or the opposite of God's blessings.

28:28 See verse 12 and note; 29:2.

29:1 *stiff-necked.* Self-willed (see 28:14b) and unteachable. *many rebukes.* See 1:30; 5:12; 9:7-8 and note; 10:17; 12:1 and note.

29:2 See 28:12 and note.

29:3 *joy to his father*. See 10:1 and note; 28:7. *squanders his wealth*. Implying that this is a disgrace and a sorrow to his father (see 6:26).

29:4 See 8:15-16 and notes; 20:8, 26.

29:5 See 26:28 and note. Here the lying smooth-talk backfires on the flatterer.

29:6 *snared by his own sin*. See 1:18.

29:7 *care about justice*. Literally "know justice;" that is, they know by understanding and doing what God requires. *concern*. Literally "knowledge," in the same sense as knowing justice.

29:8 *Mockers*. See 9:7-9 and notes. *stir up*. The unwise, by nature, are disposed to undermine harmony in society. *turn away anger*. Wisdom makes for wholesomeness and peace.

29:9 *there is no peace*. Getting into a dispute with a fool is likely to be a no-win situation. Even when the court decides the issue the fool will not be reconciled because he is incapable of rational argument.

29:10 *Bloodthirsty men*. A reminder that there are those whose perversity of character is such that their attacks on ordered society will reach extremes.

29:11 Wisdom often stresses the importance of self-control (see 12:16; 14:9, 29, 35; 20:3). There are plenty of intelligent people who show lack of wisdom by their hot tempers.

29:12 The responsibility of leadership is seen in the fact that corruption in society tends to start where there is power. The dishonest ruler will not only attract evil officials but also will corrupt others in his service.

29:13 *gives sight to the eyes of both*. A poetic way of saying that both the poor man and the oppressor are created by God (see 22:2 and note).

29:14 See verse 4; 16:12-13 and notes.

29:15 See 13:24; 22:15; 23:13-14 and notes.

29:16 The vocabulary of this saying suggests that there is an implicit understanding of the justice of God that will ultimately establish a righteous order.

29:17 *Discipline*. This is the positive effect of wisdom instruction. In the covenantal context of Israelite thought, the revelation of God is the source of discipline and instruction. God's discipline is also seen in the circumstances which he controls.

29:18 *revelation*. Literally "vision;" a word used of prophetic revelation. If there is no revelation it is either because God has given no word in some specific situation (see 1 Sam 3:1) or because there is an inability to hear what God has said (see Amos 8:11-12). *who keeps the law*. The person who does not ignore or cast off the restraints of God's word.

29:19 An observation of society rather than a fixed principle. The educational applications of wisdom are in view here, with the recognition that not all dispositions can be changed by words or reason alone.

29:20 See 26:12 and note.

29:21 *pampers*. The master neglects to exercise discipline or correction (see v. 19).

29:22 *An angry man*. The same as a hot-tempered one. There is a lack of self-control and hence an inability to respond to provocative situations in a way that is constructive (see 28:25 and note).

29:23 See 15:33; 16:18-19 and notes. Pride prevents a person from benefiting from another's wisdom.

29:24 A difficult verse that seems to draw attention to the "Catch-22" situation that a criminal accomplice faces. He is obliged to be a witness since he knows about the crime. If he refuses to witness he is held guilty (see Lev 5:1), but if he does witness he incriminates himself.

29:25 Despite appearances the power and control of events lie with God and not people. If we fear what others may say or do we attribute the maintenance of order to them. This is the opposite of trust in the Lord.

29:26 Rulers have responsibility to maintain a godly order in society and are the agents of God's rule (see 21:1; Rom 13:1-4). Human rulers, however, are sinners and never without some weaknesses in their working. The only sure justice is from God, whether it is received because of the governor's intervention or despite it.

29:27 *The righteous detest . . . the wicked detest*. Such antagonism between righteousness and wickedness is a fact of human existence. We should not be surprised when it surfaces.

9

Agur, Lemuel, and the exceptional wife Proverbs 30:1-31:31

Selected unit - Proverbs 30:1-33

Description

The problem with the editorial sub-headings in the book of Proverbs is that they show where a section begins but not necessarily where it ends. For example, it is not clear that the ascription in 30:1 covers the whole of chapter 30. However, the heading ascribing the words to Agur tells us nothing of significance about what follows, and the form and content of these sayings is far more significant than who said or wrote them.

It is not possible to say whether all the sayings in this section have a common origin since "authors" of wisdom literature almost certainly gathered material from other sources. Once again we need to confront the possible foreign origins of some of our Book of Proverbs. Agur is otherwise unknown in the Old Testament, as is Lemuel to whom at least part of chapter 31 is attributed. Lemuel is more of a problem than

Agur since he is said to be "King" (31:1) and we know of no king in Israel of that name. Again we have to recognise the principles we have discussed concerning the wisdom of Amen-em-ope (see the introduction to Chapter 7). The words of Agur in 30:2-9 contain a number of references to God or the Lord, so the passage was either written by an Israelite or adapted into the framework of Israelite faith.

There are some distinctive literary features particularly in the first part of this chapter. First, there is the unusual description of these sayings as "an oracle" (30:1), although there is some ambiguity about the meaning of this word (see the commentary on the text below). If the Hebrew word does mean oracle, it is a term used only for prophetic words, except here and in 31:1. Second, the character of these sayings is unlike most of the other material in Proverbs. One could easily understand, for example, if verse 4 were to be found in a prophetic book. Indeed, the similarities between this passage and Isaiah 40:12-16 are evident. Furthermore, the sense of mystery that surrounds the being and doing of God would be more at home in the speculative wisdom of Job or Ecclesiastes. Third, the wisdom of verse 5 and 6 enters much more into the realm of cultic worship or devotional thought than proverbial wisdom. Finally, verses 7 to 9 are a prayer to God that is quite unlike anything else in Proverbs.

Once again the form of the numerical saying is used in verses 16 to 31 and possibly in verses 11-14 (see Chapter 4). Whether these verses are to be considered as part of Agur's wisdom is not really important for our purposes. They are of quite different form and content than verses 2 to 9 but this does not preclude the possibility that one man wrote or collected the whole group.

Text

30:1-33 See note on 1:1. It is difficult, given the nature of
wisdom literature, to say how crediting of this section to Agur
fits with the opening reference to Solomon. If 1:1 is intended
to cover the whole collection then it does not necessarily
mean that Solomon is the sole author. Probably it is a way of
giving assent to the whole of Proverbs as a work that expresses
the Solomonic tradition of wisdom.

30:1 *Agur son of Jakeh.* The identity of this man is unknown
and some consider him a foreigner. If this is so, the comments
on the wisdom of Amen-em-ope apply here also (see note on
22:17-24:22). We must suppose that some Israelite has
reworked the material with a specifically Yahwistic covenant
theology (in which case it is unlikely that the credits would
have been preserved). Otherwise it is possible that Agur is a
convert to the faith of Israel. *an oracle.* See the NIV text note.
There is a possibility that the Hebrew is a place name, *Massa*
(see also 31:1), and that both Agur and Lemuel were
Ishmaelites from a town of this name that is thought to have
been in Arabia (see Gen 25:14). *Ithiel . . Ucal.* The NIV reads
this as the names of people being addressed by Agur. The
NIV text note suggests another possibility that hardly seems
to fit the context. The RSV text note is probably nearer the
mark when it says that the Hebrew is obscure.

30:2-3 This kind of reflective wisdom is not characteristic
of Proverbs and is more at home in either Job or Ecclesiastes.
There is a recognition not merely of one's own ignorance but
of the element of mystery in the being and ways of God. We
have already seen some proverbial sayings that recognise the
bounds of human wisdom. Here again is a reminder that
finite knowledge can never penetrate the depths of the mind
or being of God. There is, however, still a difficulty in the

disclaimer. In what sense has Agur not learned even the wisdom of a man? What follows in verse 4 suggests that he is mockingly comparing himself with those who think too highly of human wisdom and leave no room for the mystery of a transcendent God. In their eyes he is a fool. Such a comparison hints at Paul's exposition in 1 Corinthians 1 of the way the wisdom that comes from God is regarded by the secular mind as stupidity.

30:4 The better alternative to the boasting of the know-all is quiet submission and trust in the living God. Unlike Job 38, where God asks devastating questions to put Job in his place, here Agur asks the questions to express his conviction that empirically based knowledge can never discover God. No human being can submit God to scrutiny or emulate his creative power. *the name of his son.* The student he instructs in wisdom (see 1:8; 2:1 etc.).

30:5-6 This statement appears to come from an Israelite who is thoroughly familiar with the law and the writings of the prophets. It is possible that an Israelite editor has inserted it as a response to the recognition of mystery in verses 3 to 4. Verse 5 quotes Psalm 18:30, and verse 6a echoes Deuteronomy 4:2. Here the word of God is put forward as the basis of all true knowledge. Since it is the word of the covenant-keeping, saving God of Israel it means that to accept his word is more than the gaining of knowledge: it is salvation and life itself (see note on 1:7). On the other hand, rejection of God's word is an act of self-disqualification from the care and mercy of God. *flawless.* Tried and found to be utterly reliable. *Do not add to his words.* To add to God's words is to sit in judgment on them and to find them wanting according to human wisdom. Thus, the whole basis of knowledge and truth is shifted from God to ourselves. This is the essence of humanism and the foundation of sinful rebellion against God.

30:7-9 This section is a prayer that is not characteristic of proverbial wisdom. It reflects a desire to learn from the kind of wisdom that is in Proverbs and goes beyond the emphasis on human experience. It shows the same recognition as in Solomon's prayer (see 1 Ki 3) that it is fitting to ask for wisdom. *before I die.* There is no indication that the writer is expecting to die soon. The expression probably implies a desire to have the request granted throughout his life. *give only my daily bread.* Extremes of poverty and unnecessary riches both need to be avoided. One leads to dishonesty out of desperation (v. 9b) and the other to lack of reliance on the provision of the Lord (v. 9a; see Dt 8:10-18; Lk 12:16-21).

30:10 An incomplete instruction that seems to have no real connection with what precedes or follows. It is a warning against becoming involved in the household affairs of other people.

30:11-14 It is possible that this section once began with a numerical formula similar to verses 15b, 18, 21 and 29 (see note on 6:16-19). If not a listing of those who earn God's judgment, these sayings come close to being a joining of wisdom thought to a prophetic utterance so as to make a direct condemnation of certain sins. *curse . . . do not bless.* See 20:20 and note. *pure in their own eyes.* See 16:2; 21:2 and notes.

30:15a This is not part of the numerical saying that follows, but it is probably placed here because of the thematic similarity with it. *Give! Give!* As the leech sucks blood voraciously, so its offspring are insatiable. This seems to be a metaphor for the fact that greed breeds greed.

30:15b-16 See notes on 6:16-19. The common theme is the insatiable appetite (see 15a and note).

30:17 *The eye that mocks.* A contemptuous look can be as poisonous as words. Wisdom shows affinity with the law in its condemnation of those who dishonour and despise their parents. The breakdown of the most fundamental human relationship deserves the strongest curse: the offender would lie unburied and have his offending eye eaten by carrion birds.

30:18-19 For the numerical form see notes on 6:16-19. The four "ways" cannot be understood because they leave no traces, or because they are so easily yet mysteriously mastered. Some commentators suppose the emphasis to be on the fourth way, human sexuality, of which the other three would be metaphors.

30:20 Not part of the previous saying but probably placed here as a contrast with it. *She eats and wipes her mouth.* A metaphor for sexual intercourse; her adultery has become as natural to her as eating. *I've done nothing wrong.* All moral sense has been suppressed.

30:21-23 See note on 6:16-19. *the earth trembles.* The four items in verse 22 and 23 hardly seem able to produce such dire consequences even if we regard them as meaning the disruption of the social order. It is possible that such disorders are linked somehow with natural disaster, but it is more likely that this is hyperbole for an intolerable state of affairs.

30:24-28 See note on 6:16-19. If this saying were purely an observation on natural history it would still fulfil one of the functions of wisdom: the perception of order and of how things relate. Many nature proverbs show concern for nature as a parable of human life (e.g. 6:6-11). The fact that wisdom is ascribed to these creatures implies some unity with human existence. The creatures are wise because they are able to surmount some serious inherent weakness so as to survive well.

30:29-31 See note on 6:16-19. The inclusion of a king among the animals suggests human parallels with nature and the underlying coherence of all creation. Such parallels do not necessarily mean that we have to search for the moral lesson of the saying. The mere observation of rule and order in both animal and human society is not without significance.

30:32 *clap your hand over your mouth*. Stop talking; that is, cease your scheming and provocation.

30:33 *churning . . . twisting . . . stirring up*. Literally, Hebrew has "pressing" in each case, thus emphasising the parallel feature in each situation. In this saying we have a warning that pushing provocation too far leads to strife, even to bloodied noses.

Function

The precise literary function of these sayings is hard to pin down. It may be that the editor responsible for the final form of Proverbs has gathered these miscellaneous pieces together and placed them at the end of the book. Perhaps he did it for no other reason than the difficulty of including them within the more empirical wisdom of the instructions and proverbial sentences.

However, we cannot separate the literary question from the theological. The instructions and proverbial sentences lend themselves readily to the empirical wisdom that concentrates on the experiences of life and the lessons to be learned from them. They are a means to understanding the nature of the order in reality that makes it possible to build a sense of purpose, of right and wrong, and of having some responsibility for the way we live. Scattered throughout the empirical wisdom of Proverbs are explicitly theological sayings that remind us that the sages regarded themselves as children of the covenant promises of God. They recognise not only that true wisdom must begin with the revealed wisdom of God, but also that there are limits to human wisdom. This is the emphasis in verses 2 to 6.

The function of the numerical sayings, which may include verses 7 to 9, is another matter. They undoubtedly fit more into empirical wisdom than into speculative or theological wisdom. They seem to link with the making of lists in which some kind of classification is involved (see Chapter 4).

Testimony to Christ

Agur's question in verse 4 is answered directly in Jesus' reply to Nicodemus in John 3:13, "No one has ever gone into heaven except the one who came from heaven - the Son of Man." We are required by this application to enquire why Jesus uses it. The fact that it is a response to Proverbs 30:4 helps to settle the apparent difficulty in John 3:13. Jesus is not implying that the Son of Man had to first go to heaven from earth and then to come down again. The point is that heaven is the place where the deep wisdom of God is found and only the Man from heaven has had access to such wisdom. Proverbs 30:2-4 is primarily a testimony to the inability of sinful humans to plumb the mysteries of God and of the ultimate meaning of our existence. Since the implied answer is "nobody" we should beware of reading more than is really there into the reference to the son (v. 4; see text comment above). While it so happens that the one who does bring heavenly wisdom is the Son of Man, this passage gives negative testimony to that fact.

There is a more direct connection between the next saying (vv. 5-6) and Christ as the word and wisdom of God. Ultimate wisdom is in Jesus who is the revealer of God and the embodiment of God's wisdom (see Jn 1:1-18; 1 Cor 1:18-2:16). Once again we are reminded that the wisdom in the Old Testament recognised the priority of God's wisdom as the foundation for all human wisdom. The gospel takes this up and shows that God's saving revelation in Christ is the key to all reality. The development of a truly Christian mind-set is not merely to take on board a lot of Christian doctrine, as important as that is. It also involves the interpretation of life and events in the light of the person and work of Christ. The numerical sayings, fitting as they do into empirical wisdom, testify in a general way to the humanity which Christ came to restore. All empirical wisdom reflects the cultural mandate given to Adam and Eve in the Garden and not rescinded after the fall. Christ's perfect humanity included his perfect expression of human wisdom by which our feeble and sin-clouded wisdom is justified and accounted acceptable to God.

Questions

1. What do you see as the main message in verses 2 to 4?

2. What kind of wisdom is referred to in verses 5 to 6?

3. What does verse 15a have in common with verses 15b and 16?

4. What do you consider to be the lesson of each of the numerical sayings in this section?

Comments on Proverbs 31:1-9

31:1 *The sayings of King Lemuel - an oracle.* See note on 30:1. Lemuel is not an Israelite king. The nature of this section (vv. 1-9) strongly suggests an Egyptian or perhaps a Babylonian origin. Its intention is apparently vocational, the equipping of the ruler for his task. The form is similar to the instructions of chapters 1-9 (see the introduction in Chapter 4). Lemuel was instructed by his mother. While the father may have been the principal teacher of the children, godly women often took that role (see 1:8). There were in Israel certain wise women of significance (e.g. 2 Sam 14:2; 20:16).

31:2 *son of my womb.* Probably a term of endearment. *son of my vows.* There may have been a vow made in anticipation of the birth (as Hannah made a vow in 1 Sam 1:11).

31:3 *those who ruin kings.* By involving them in immoral behaviour and distracting them from their God-ordained task of ruling wisely.

31:4-5 *It is .. not for kings to drink wine.* The king was responsible for the welfare of all his people; he must not become besotted with wine and thus unable to do his duties.

31:6-7 *Give beer . . . wine to those who are in anguish.* While strong drink may wreak havoc in the execution of kingly duties it may, on the other hand, have a palliative effect on those who are suffering.

31:8-9 The duties of a king under the covenant are referred to in Deuteronomy 17:14-20. Here the king's task is designated as upholding righteousness in society and having a special concern for the underprivileged.

Selected unit - Proverbs 31:10-31

Description

This is an acrostic which constructs the Hebrew alphabet from the initial letter of each line. Similar alphabetic devices are found in Psalms 9; 10; 25; 34; 37; 111; 112; 119 (using the first letter of each section of eight verses); 145; Lamentations 1 to 4; and several other places. One possible explanation for the device is that it served as an aid to memorising of the passage.

This poem is in praise of the good wife, who exemplifies the principles of wisdom both in practical and spiritual terms. The demands of getting the poem into the alphabetical acrostic – no mean feat – may explain why there is no clear progression of thought. The general effect, though, is a coherent, if rather idealistic, description of a woman beautified by her wisdom in the practical matters of the home and family. The household in question appears to by quite well off, but this does not detract from the universal applicability of the principles of wifely wisdom.

Text

31:10 *who can find?* This is not an impossible dream, but such a wife is sufficiently rare to require a diligent search. *worth far more than rubies.* In addition to the obvious significance of this comparison, there may well be the idea that the woman is the embodiment of wisdom that is often compared with precious metals and stones (e.g. 1:9; 2:4; 3:15; Job 28:1-19).

31:11 *lacks nothing of value.* The wife's astuteness in managing the affairs of the household ensures the prosperity they enjoy.

31:12 *good . . . all the days of her life.* These are the benefits of wisdom in that it promotes life and avoids all that threatens it (see 18:22).

31:13 *eager hands.* Literally "pleasure of her hands." She works with a will because it is no drudgery to her.

31:14 *like the merchant ships.* Verse 18 indicates the wife's skill at trading. *bringing her food from afar.* Not so much a shopping excursion to some distant store, but rather the ability to find new ways of adding to the family finances.

31:15 There is some obscurity in this verse. Both the NIV and RSV have opted for a translation that indicates that the wife oversees the feeding of her family and of the servants, perhaps to see that it is done properly and without waste. Another possibility is that the reference is to household duties so that the household is well organised and efficiently run from the beginning of each day.

31:16 The wife is an astute business woman and reinvests her earnings.

31:17 *her arms are strong.* There is wisdom in the profitable use of one's physical capabilities.

31:18 *her trading is profitable.* She is able to engage in trade and turn an honest profit. *her lamp does not go out.* This is either a metaphor for prosperity, as in 13:9, or a reference to the wife's diligence in using the hours of dark for work.

31:19 *the distaff.* The Hebrew is uncertain. Both the NIV and RSV have "distaff" which is a stick used in spinning by hand or a part of a spinning wheel. The context indicates that the wife has the skill to make her own thread.

31:20 *She opens her arms to the poor.* She exemplifies the principle that prosperity is meant to be shared with those who are less well off (see Eph 4:28).

31:21 *scarlet.* The Hebrew is uncertain. The same letters can be read to mean "double," which suggests that the family members are clothed in adequate protection from the cold.

31:22 Bedding and clothing are of good quality.

31:23 The implication is that the wife's efficiency in running the household releases her husband from any domestic and financial concerns so that he is free to give time to public life. The woman is the power behind the social structures of good order. *city gate.* See 1:21 and note.

31:24 See verse 18 and note.

31:25 Either the wife shows great strength and dignity of character or, more likely in view of the second line, she is economically secure and has no concerns for the future. Both are consistent with wisdom.

31:26-27 *faithful instruction.* The wife has wisdom to impart to those in the household, both in ordinary conversation and in deliberate instruction. This is part of her obligation as a wife, mother and employer. *the bread of idleness.* There is no prosperity from idleness.

31:28-29 The result of the wife's skill is the cementing of family relationships. The praise of husband and children is her great reward.

31:30-31 *who fears the Lord.* See 1:7 and note. Up to this point the poem is secular in tone and concentrates on practical wisdom. Now, as in 1:7, the basis of all true wisdom is referred to. This is a fitting end to the Book of Proverbs for it brings us back to the starting point and the principle underlying all true wisdom. Practical wisdom which people gain apart from God's revelation may be valid up to a point, but only the fear of the Lord, a trusting and faithful response to God's word, can provide the basis for knowing what life is about and what meaning we have. The fear of the Lord is the foundation of wisdom as we learn to interpret reality through the revelation of God. It is also the goal of wisdom as we come to know more of the reality of our God. *the reward she has earned.* Not salvation by works, but the normal outcome of the good and wise life. *praise at the city gate.* The wife has a good reputation among the counsellors who gather at the gate and, possibly, she is herself numbered among them.

Function

There is little reason to suppose that this poem is simply a kind of allegory extolling wisdom in the abstract, even though wisdom is often spoken of as a woman (e.g. 1:20; 8:1; 9:1-6). Even if the editor did not intend it, this section has an important balancing effect by dealing with the virtues of a wise woman. Much of the moral teaching in the instructions is directed at young men, warning them of the immoral woman (e.g. 5:1-14; 6:20-35; 7:1-27). There are also references in the sentence literature to the quarrelsome wife (19:13; 21:9; 25:24; 27:15). Social conditions in the Ancient Near East may well have dictated the predominant concern for the education of young men in the skills of life and community service. While Israel was not elitist in its educational concerns in the way the Egyptians seem to have been, there was nevertheless an emphasis on the role of the men.

This poem of the wise woman is notable for its unstinting praise of the woman and also for the unquestioning acceptance of the rightness of this woman's achievements. They are not solely domestic, though her guidance and influence in the home is portrayed as both welcome and as having extensive benefits. It would appear that she is a good wife and mother, even the ideal homemaker, while engaging in some form of commercial activity as a career. The skill and wisdom with which she combines the two functions commend her to the community so that she may well have a ministry as a counsellor.

In more general terms we can see this poem functioning as a fitting conclusion to a book that takes an optimistic view of life when it is lived in the fear of the Lord. It is optimistic about the possibility of learning to live wisely and to avoid evil and folly. It says that there is great gain and much satisfaction in living when we take the trouble to learn and to practise wisdom. The wise woman is the paragon of practical wisdom and consequently she embodies the teaching of Proverbs in a real-life situation that is praiseworthy, satisfying, productive and generally beneficial to herself and to others.

Testimony to Christ

At first sight it may seem forced to be suggesting that a poem about a wise women testifies to Christ. We need, however, to remind ourselves that the teaching of Jesus is that the whole of the Scripture testifies to him. That point is settled. So the question for us is how a particular section testifies to Christ.

To make any sort of real progress in the matter we need to start by asking how the particular text functioned in its own theological context as a testimony to the saving work of God. Proverbs starts with the theological assertion that the fear of Lord is the starting point in the quest for true knowledge and wisdom. It ends with a statement about a woman who fears the Lord (31:30). This statement sums up the significance of the woman who is the subject of the poem and applies it to any woman who fears the Lord and thus learns wisdom.

As we have reflected on each of the selected passages and on their testimony to Christ, our concern has been to uncover the principles that will enable us to read Proverbs as Christian Scripture. We have seen that all true human wisdom proceeds within the framework of the revealed wisdom of God that is his redemptive plan. The Israelite had to understand life and the meaning of things in the light of God's revealed purposes for his fallen creation. The plan of salvation embraces the whole of creation and shows its origins, its purposes, its sin-induced sicknesses, its healing and its final destiny. Within that framework is the day-to-day living of ordinary people. Many strive for excellence apart from God and may seem to achieve it for a while. Others are turned around by the grace of God from a pathway that may seem straight for a time but that ultimately leads to destruction. They learn that the fear of the Lord is the only sure foundation for everyday life and for human relationships.

In New Testament terms, the wise woman of Proverbs 31 shows a specific example of redemption's effect on life. The fear of the Lord translates into faith in Christ. He is the true wisdom of God and of humankind. Being the wisdom of God, he implements the perfect plan of salvation that is bringing in the kingdom of God. Being the wisdom of humankind, he justifies our imperfect and often unbelieving wisdom so that we are no longer condemned for our failures and folly. We are thus set free in him to pursue the task of intellectual and practical sanctification.

Questions

1. In the teaching about the good wife, what do you think merely reflects ancient Israelite culture? What expresses wisdom to be desired by all?

2. Could this teaching be applied to any member of the family or only a wife?

3. How does all this practical wisdom relate to the fear of the Lord?

Further reading

Alden, Robert L., *Proverbs: A Commentary on an Ancient Book of Timeless Advice* (Grand Rapids: Baker Book House, 1983). A verse-by-verse exegetical commentary.

Hubbard, David A., *Proverbs (The Communicator's Commentary*, Dallas: Word Books, 1989). An exegetical and thematic treatment.

Goldsworthy, Graeme, *Proverbs* (*Bible Probe*, London: Scripture Union, 1989). A mini-commentary designed as a study book for small groups.

Kidner, Derek, *Proverbs*, (*Tyndale Commentary*, Leicester: Inter-Varsity Press, 1964). The thematic approach to each section makes it less accessible as an exegetical tool. In addition to the exegetical commentary there are a number of subject studies and a useful concordance of key words.

McKane, William, *Proverbs: A New Approach*, (*Old Testament Library*, Philadelphia: The Westminster Press, 1970). Contains an extensive introduction to the international wisdom literature of the Ancient Near East. A technical commentary which proposes a particular thesis on the development of Israelite wisdom literature.

Mouser, William E., *Walking in Wisdom: Studying the Proverbs of Solomon*, (Downers Grove: InterVarsity Press, 1983). The author's aim is to unlock the meaning of Proverbs through an analysis of the various types of parallelism and other literary devices.

Woodcock, Eldon, *Proverbs: A Topical Study* (*Bible Study Commentary Series*, Grand Rapids: Lamplighter Books, Zondervan, 1988). The material is arranged according to leading topics. A useful source of main themes and their treatment but not so helpful as an exegetical commentary.